MW00622764

William Whiston's 1727 Pioneering
Translation of

Extracts out of

The Book of Enoch

Including:

*His Rigorous Defense of the Book of
Enoch as a Legitimate Part of the Bible*

Also by Whiston:

Testaments of
Twelve Patriarchs

The 21st Century Edition of

William Whiston's 1727 Pioneering
Translation of

Extracts out of

The Book of Enoch

Including:

His Rigorous Defense of the Book of
Enoch as a Legitimate Part of the Bible

Also by Whiston:

Testaments of
Twelve Patriarchs

R.I. Burns, Editor

SageWorks Press
2023

First KDP print edition, April, 2023 ~ rev. 5/27/23
San Francisco, CA USA
ISBN: 978-1-68564-451-2

Cover Art: Jonathan Bowling

Thank you, Paul Bruce, for extraordinary proofing.

www.TheBookofEnoch.info

Dedicated to all futurist, end-times, enthusiasts, throughout the world! Watch and pray!

"He who devotes himself to the study of the law of the Most High will seek out the wisdom of all the ancients, and will be concerned with prophecies; he will preserve the discourse of notable men and penetrate the subtleties of parables; he will seek out the hidden meanings of proverbs and be at home with the obscurities of parables." ~ Ecclesiasticus 39:1-3

EXTRACTS

OUT OF THE

First Book of *Enoch,*

CONCERNING

The *Egregori:* [or *fallen Angels.*]

Out of Syncellus' Chronograph, Cap. II

Translated into ENGLISH.

By W i l l i a m W h i s t o n, M.A.
Sometime Professor of the Mathematicks in the
University of *Cambridge.*

L O N D O N:
Printed for the author: and are to be Sold By
the Booksellers of *London* and *Westminster.*
A.D. MDCCXXVII.

Preface to the
21ˢᵗ-Century Edition.

William Whiston, the sometime friend and colleague of Sir Isaac Newton, succeeded Newton as Lucasian Professor of Mathematics at Cambridge. However, it was more than a passion for Physics and Mathematics which Whiston and Newton shared. These two scientists were also enthusiastic believers in the Bible as the revelation of God's word. Besides this, they were both also fans of a speculative, futurist, study of the Biblical subject of the end-times.

This is especially significant in our time, in which, increasingly, many Bible-believing Christians are adopting anti-futurist opinions about Bible prophecy. It is often assumed in our day that the futurist perspective on Bible prophecy is a modern, American, creation. Futurist eschatology is frequently *blamed* on the likes of John Nelson Darby and C. I. Scofield. Yet, in Sir Isaac Newton and in William Whiston we have two European, academes, staking out a futurist perspective on the end-times. Bear in mind, this was before there was anything one might call a specifically "American" identity. At that time, the Great Awakening was a decade away, Benjamin Franklin, Jonathan Edwards, and John Wesley were in their early 20's, George Whitefield was a teenager and George Washington was yet to be born.

It seemed fitting then, to include here two of William Whiston's translations of books which Whiston believed to be legitimate Scriptures which had become alienated from the Bible. The two books included in this volume are both of that Biblical genre known as "apocalypse". Apocalypses uniquely lend themselves to a futurist perspective of Bible prophecy.

Both the *Book of Enoch,* and its counterpart the *Testaments of the Twelve Patriarchs* are *apocalypses* which claim to pull back the veil on the unseen realm of spiritual realities, often claiming to reveal events yet future. Since Whiston's rationale for the validity of the *Book of Enoch,* relies heavily upon the *Testaments of the Twelve Patriarchs,* the *Testaments* are included here for reference. The *Testaments* themselves repeatedly make the internal claim that the *Book of Enoch* was used by the patriarchs to gain insight into future events.

Though William Whiston is a passionate proponent of the authenticity of *Enoch,* the one great obstacle to this research in his day, was that *Enoch's* book was considered lost, except for a few Greek fragments. These Greek fragments come down to us from the hand of the 9th century chronographer, *George Syncellus.*

It is hoped that this 21st century edition of these two Whiston works will contribute to the fast-growing field of *Enoch*ic studies, as well as help revive appreciation for Whiston's long-forgotten work.

R.I. Burns,
Pacifica, California
March 19, 2021

To the reader:
In reprinting Whiston's works, effort was made to retain as much as possible of the look and feel for the original. English prose 300 years ago was quite different than that of today. To prevent the unwelcome alteration of Whiston's meaning, most but not all archaic word forms were left unchanged as well.

Introduction to the 21st Century Edition.

Readers of William Whiston's translation of Greek fragments of the *Book of Enoch*, may be surprised by his enthusiasm for it all. Whiston's excitement for this subject comes through in his writings as much today as we imagine it did in his own era, three centuries ago.

As has been mentioned, both William Whiston and his friend and colleague, Sir *Isaac* Newton, were avid Bible students, and both men shared a particular fondness for the topic of the end-times in the Bible.

One might assume then, that investigating the *Book of Enoch* would be a logical step for Whiston, since by anyone's estimate, the *Book of Enoch* stands today as perhaps *the most important* pre-Christian apocalypse of all. However, in 1727, William Whiston did not possess any of the apocalyptic portions of the *Book of Enoch!* Despite this limitation, Whiston was able to perceive worth in *Enoch's* book just as Christians had done in ancient times...

During the first four centuries of Christianity, the Book of *Enoch* was universally available and used. However, by the time of Augustine and Jerome, in the beginning of the 5th century, the book was increasingly spoken against and removed from churches. Eventually all known copies within Western and Eastern Christianity were either lost or destroyed. In Whiston's era then, all that was available in the West were a few Greek fragments. Notably missing from the portions available to Whiston is the first chapter from the *Book of Enoch* which promises the blessings of the book to be revealed to those living in the end of times. It is from this section that Jude, the brother of Jesus, would later quote. One can only guess what Whiston would have thought had he possessed the futurist-tinged portions of the opening preamble to *Enoch*'s book! However, it would not be until a century later that a complete copy of the *Book of Enoch* would become available in the West.

In this, the 21ˢᵗ century re-publication of Whiston's, *Extracts Out of the First Book of Enoch,* and *The Testaments of the Twelve Patriarchs,* the reader will be able to enjoy not only William Whiston's translation work, but also his excited advocacy for the acceptance of the *Book of Enoch* as authentic.

When we published *The Book of Enoch Messianic Prophecy Edition,* in 2017, we noted that the *Book of Enoch,* has been going through a gradual process of reemergence on the world scene. With this re-release of Whiston's work, we hope to help shine a light on an overlooked chapter in that process and in the rediscovery of the *Book of Enoch* in our modern world.

In the following pages, the reader is invited to enjoy as William Whiston seeks…

> *"…to prove that this Book of Enoch, was really genuine, and was one of the Sacred Apocryphal or Concealed Books of the Old Testament".*

EXTRACTS

OUT OF THE

First Book of *Enoch,*

CONCERNING

The *Egregori:* [or *fallen Angels.*]

Out of Syncellus' Chronograph, *Cap.* II

I.

I. **A**ND it came to pass when the Children of Men were multiplied, beautiful Daughters were born to them: and the *Egregori* coveted them, and went astray after them: and said, one to the other, Let us choose to our selves wives from the Daughters of Men which are on the Earth. And *Semiazas,* their *Archon,* [*or President*] said unto them, I am fearful that you will not do this thing, and I alone shall be guilty of this great Sin. And they answered him, and said, Let every one of us swear with an oath; and let us bind one another under a curse, that we will not alter this our purpose, until we have performed it. Then they all swore together, and bound one another under a curse. Now they were two hundred that descended, in the Days of *Jared,* upon the top of the Mountain of

Hermonim. And they called the mountain *Hermon,* from the oath they had taken, and the curse they had bound one another withal upon it. These are the Names of their *Archontes; (1.) Semiazas, their President. (2.) Atarcuph. (3.) Arakiel. (4.) Chobabiel. (5.) Orammane. (6.) Ramiel. (7.) Sampsich. (8.) Zakiel. (9.) Balkiel. (10.) Azalzel. [Azael.] (11.) Pharmaros. (12.) Amariel. (13.) Anagemas. (14.) Thausael. (15.) Samiel. (16.) Sarinas (17.) Eumiel. (18.) Tyriel. (19.) Jumiel. (20.) Sariel.*

II. These, and all the rest, in the 1170th year of the world, took to themselves wives, and began to defile themselves with them, until the Flood: and they bear to them three sorts, [*as their posterity,*] The first were the great *Giants.* Now the *Giants* begat the *Naphilim,* and the *Eliudim* were born to the *Naphilim.* And they increased in their bulk, and they taught one another, and one another's wives, witchcrafts, and charms. *Azael* was the first, but the tenth of the *Archontes;* and He taught men to make swords, and breastplates, and all sorts of armour, and metals out of the Earth; and how they might work in gold, and silver, and make them ornaments for their wives. He taught them also to burnish, and to paint their Faces, and the use of precious stones, and of washes. And the Sons of Men made these things for themselves, and for their Daughters. And they transgressed, and made the Saints to go astray. And there was great Impiety upon the Earth: and they perverted their ways. Moreover, their chief Archon *Semiazas* taught them to have a spite against the mind, [*or remedies efficacious against diseases,*] and the roots of herbs that were in the Earth. But *Pharmaros*, the eleventh, taught witchcrafts, charms, cunning arts, and the dissolution of charms. The ninth taught them Astroscopy; the fourth taught Astrology; and the eighth taught Aeroscopy; and the third taught the Signs of the Earth; and the seventh taught the Signs of the Sun; and the twentieth taught the Signs of Moon. All these began to reveal these Mysteries to their Wives and to their Children.

III. Now, afterwards, the *Giants* began to devour the Flesh of Men, and mankind began to be diminished upon the Earth. And the remainder cried unto Heaven, on account of their affliction, desiring that their Memorial might be carried up before the Lord......

IV. And when the four great Archangels, *Michael*, and *Uriel*, and *Raphael*, and *Gabriel* heard thereof, they looked down out of the holy places of Heaven, and saw a great deal of blood shed upon the Earth, and all kind of impiety and wickedness practiced; They came in [*again,*] and said to one another, that the Spirits and Souls of Men groan, and intercede, and say, Introduce our prayer before the Most High, and our woeful estate before the glory of the [*Divine*] Majesty, before Him who in greatness is Lord of all Lords. And the four Archangels came near, and said to the Lord of the world, Thou art the God of Gods, and the Lord of Lords, and the King of Kings. and the God of mankind; and the Throne of thy glory is through all the generations of eternity: and thy name is Holy, and Blessed for ever and ever.

Apoc. VI. 9, 10.
VIII. 3, 4.
Tob. xii. 15.

For thou art He who hast made all things, and hast the power over all things; and all things are manifest and open before thee, and thou seest all things, and there is nothing that can be hid from thee. Thou seest what *Azael* has done, and what he has introduced, and what he has taught; there is nothing but injustice and wickedness upon the Earth, and all kind of deceit upon the dry Land. For he has taught the mysteries, and has revealed to the world the things of Heaven. They follow his Counsels. The Sons of Men aim to know the Mysteries. Thou hast given power to *Semiazas* to have the Assistance of those that are with him: they have gone after the Daughters of Men on the Earth, and have lain with them, and are defiled with females; and they have discovered to them all their sinful practices, and have taught them to do things abominable. And now, behold, the Daughters of Men have born children to them, even the *Giants*. Perverse things are diffused over the Earth; and the whole Earth is full of injustice. And now, behold, the Spirits of the Souls of the Men that are dead intercede and their groaning is come up to the gates of Heaven: nor can they depart, because of the acts of violence that are committed upon the Earth. And thou knowest these things before they are done, and seest these [*Egregori*] and sayest nothing. What is to be done in this Matter?

V. Then the Most High said; and He that is Holy, He that is Great, spake; and sent *Uriel* to the Son of *Lamech*, saying, Go thou to *Noe*, and say unto him, in my Name, Hide thyself: and declare to him the End that is coming: for the Earth shall entirely perish: and say to him, that there shall come a Deluge upon all the Earth, to destroy everything from the face of the Earth. Teach that just one, the Son of *Lamech*, what he shall do, and thereby preserve his Soul in Life, and shall escape for ever; and a flock shall arise from him, and shall be established for all generations, to the end of the world.

VI. And he said to *Raphael*, Go, *Raphael*, and bind *Azael*; tie him hands and feet, and cast him into the darkness, and open the desert that is in the desert of *Dudael*, and go and cast him thither, and lay under him sharp and rugged Stones, and cover him with darkness, and let him dwell there for ever, and obstruct his light, and let him not see light. And at the day of Judgment he shall be led away to the burning fire. And heal the Earth, which the *Egregori* have destroyed, and discover the method of healing that plague, that they may cure that plague; and that all the Sons of Men may not perish by the mystery which the *Egregori* have discovered, and have taught it to their Sons; and all the Earth is laid waste by the works of the doctrine of *Azael*: and to it do thou ascribe all the Sins [*they have committed.*]

VII. And He said unto *Gabriel*, Go, *Gabriel*, to the *Giants*, that spurious breed, to the Sons of fornication, and destroy the Sons of the *Egregori*, from the Sons of Men. Send them to fight one against another, by war and destruction; and they shall not have length of days and their Fathers shall have no [*room for*] intercession for them, though they promise

Tob. viii. 3.

See San-choniatho's Account of these mutual Slaughters

5

them an eternity of life, and the light of the light until 500 years.

VIII. And He said unto *Michael*, Go, *Michael*, bind *Semiazas*, and those others with him, that have mixed themselves with the Daughters of Men, so as to be defiled with them, in their impurity. And when their Sons are slain, and they have seen the perdition of their beloved, bind them for 70 generations, in the recesses of the Earth, until the day of their judgment, until the day of the completion or their end, until the judgment of eternity be fulfilled. Then shall they be led away into the *Chaos of Fire*, and into torment, and into the prison of their eternal restraint. And whomever shall be condemned, and destroyed from this time with them, shall be bound, until the completion of their generation....

IX. And now, as to the *Giants*, which were begotten of Spirits and Flesh, they shall call them Evil Spirits upon the Earth; because their habitation is upon the Earth. Spirits that are gone out of the body of their flesh, because they were derived from Men, and from the *Egregori* whence was the beginning of their Creation, and the beginning or their foundation; they will be Evil Spirits upon the Earth, the first Spirits of the *Giants*, that will be voracious and unjust, and destructive, will fall upon men, and struggle with them, and throw them upon the ground, and make incursions upon them, and will eat nothing, but continue without food, and cause spectres, thirsting, and rushing upon Men. And the Spirits shall arise against the Sons of Men and of Women, because they went out of them. It will also come to pass, that from the day of the time of the slaughter, and destruction, and death of the *Giants*, that the *Naphilim*, and the Strong of the Earth, [*the Eliudim*] those great Men of renown, the Spirits that proceed out of their Soul, as out of the flesh, shall be destroyers without distinction; they shall destroy thus until the day of their consummation, until the great Judgment, when the Great Age shall be finished, shall be all at once finished....

X. But as to the Mountain on which they swore, and bound one another under a curse, there shall never depart from it Cold, and Snow, and Frost; and Dew shall never descend upon it, unless it descend upon it for a curse, until the day of the great Judgment. At that time it shall be burnt up, and laid low, and it shall be burning and melting away, as wax by the fire; so shall it be burnt up, and all its fruits shall wither away. And now I say unto you, ye Sons of Men, that there is great wrath against your Sons, and this wrath shall not cease from you, until the time of the slaughter of your Sons; and your beloved shall perish and those you honour shall die from off the whole Earth. For all the days of their life, from this time, shall not be more than 120 Years. And do not you think that you shall still live more years; for from this time they shall have no way of escaping, because of the wrath which is kindled against you in the King of all Ages. Do not you imagine, that you shall escape these Judgments.... [*'These things,* says Syncellus, *are* *taken out of the first Book of Enoch, concerning the Egregori'.]*

****

Out of Alexander Polyhistor apud Syncell. P. 33

IN the 165th Year of *Enoch*, which was the 1286th from the Creation of the world, by the permission of the Supreme God, the Archangel *Uriel*, who was over the Stars, discovered to *Enoch* what the Month was, and the Tropick, and the Year: as it is related in the Book of the same *Enoch*: and that the Year contained 52 Weeks: and that 1286 Years contained 46 Myriads of Days, and 9390 [469390:] and six Myriads of weeks, and 7056 [67056] [*at 365 Days of the Year*] wherein Mankind knew, neither the Month, nor the Tropicks, nor the Year; nor what were each of their measures.

N. B. What Foundations of Astrology were now learned by the Discovery of the XII Signs, and 360 Degrees of the *Zodiak*, as distinct from the Length of the Month, and the Year, for the uses of the Calendar, are, by *Polyhistor*, ascribed to the 4th Archon; in these Words, preserved by *Syncellus*: 'They were taught by the 4th Archon   *p. 321* of the *Egregori*, *Chobabiel*, that the Measure of the Revolution of the Sun was in XII Signs of the *Zodiak*, and in 360 Degrees. Which must   *Enoch, 5.2* most probably be taken from *Enoch* who expressly makes this fourth Archon the Teacher of *Astrology*.

A
DISSERTATION,

T O P R O V E,

That this Book of Enoch, whose Fragments we have here produced, was really genuine, and was one of the Sacred Apocryphal or Concealed Books of the Old Testament.

THE Reasons of this Proposition, taken from the *internal Characters*, and *external Testimonies*, are these that follow.

(1.) The Case of this Book, as well as of the Testaments of the XII *Patriarchs*, is very peculiar. For if once it appear they were either of them written at all before the Christian Religion came into the World; nay, if they were either of them written at all before the Destruction of *Jerusalem* by *Titus*, they must, for certain, be genuine: because the Predictions contained in them both, are so many, and so plain, and so evidently agree to the Events that concerned the Jewish Nation, and the Christian Religion, as late as the Destruction of *Jerusalem*, that they could not probably be derived from anything else than Divine Revelation. Now since the entire Evidence, internal as well as external, conspires to assure us, that both this book of *Enoch*, and the Testaments of the XII *Patriarchs* were written before, nay, long before the Destruction of *Jerusalem* by *Titus* & as will appear all along; we ought to allow them both to be truly genuine.

(2.) The Account *Moses* gives us of the *Sons of God* conversing with the *Daughters of Men*: (for

10

so the Text was by all Jews and Christians read and understood in the first, and by almost all of them in several following Centuries:) with its Consequence, the Procreation of the *Antediluvian Giants*, seems little more than an Epitome of the larger original Account of the same thing in the book of *Enoch*; which, in this part, is pretty entirely preserved in the foregoing Fragments: as the following Parallelism will abundantly inform us.

Idolat §.9. De Cult. Fem. §. 10. Advers. Marcion. L. V. §.18. De Veland Virg. §. 7. De Hab. Mulich. §. 2. Euseb. Prep. V.4. August. De Civit: Dei

Phil. de Gygant. Joseph. Antiq. I.3. Just. Apol. I.5. II.6 Clem. Alex. Strom. III. P.450. V.p. 550. Athe- nag. Apol. §. 22. Tertull. De.

MOSES.	ENOCH.
* *It came to pass when Men began to multiply on the face of the Earth, and Daughters were born unto them, that the Sons of God [MS. Alex. Phil. Joseph. Jude,] saw the Daughters of Men, that they were fair: and they took them wives of all which they chose. And the Lord said, My Spirit shall not always strive with Man: for that ha also is flesh; yet his*	† *It came to pass when the Children of Men were multiplied, beautiful Daughters were Born to them; and the Egregori coveted them, and went astray after them. And they said one to another, [200 in Number] let us choose to ourselves wives from the Daughters of Men which are on the Earth, – They took to themselves Wives and began to defile themselves with them. [See the Manner in the Testament of Ruben, §. 5. and the like Attempt in Tob. vi. 14.3] until the Flood: and they bear to them three sorts; the first were the Giants: the Giants begat the Nephilim: and the Eliudim were bore to the Nephilim. – And they transgressed, and made the Saints to go astray. And there was great impiety upon the.*

* Gen. vi. I.——6. † Enoch §.I.

|| Sons of God: MS. Vat. Heb. §. 2.

Ibid.

Days shall an hundred and twenty years. There were Giants in the Earth in those days; and also after that, when the Sons of God [the Children of Seth] came in unto the Daughters of Men, and bear Children unto them: The same became mighty Men, which were of old, Men of renown. And God saw that the Wickedness of Man was great in the Earth; and that every imagination of the thoughts of his heart was only evil continually. And it repented the Lord that he had made Man in the Earth and it grieved him at his Heart, &c.

Earth, and they perverted their ways. – Now afterwards the. Giants began to devour the flesh of Men; and mankind began to be diminished upon the Earth. – The Egregori have gone after the Daughters of Men on the Earth, and have lain with them, and are defiled with females: and they have discovered to them all their sinful practices, and have taught them to do things abominable. And now, behold, the Daughters of Men have born Children to them, even the Giants; perverse things are diffused over the Earth; and the whole Earth is full of injustice. And now, behold, the Spirits of the Souls of Men that are dead intercede – And now I say unto you, ye Sons of men, that there is great wrath against you, and against your Sons: and this wrath shall not cease from you until the time of the slaughter of your Sons; and your beloved shall perish, and those you honour shall die from of the whole Earth; for all the Days of their Life, from this time, fall be not more than an hundred and twenty Years; And do not you think that you shall live more Years: for from this time they shall have no way of escaping, because of the wrath which is

§. 3.

§. 4.

§. 10.

12

kindled against you in the King of all Ages. Do not you imagine that you shall escape these Judgments, &c.

N.B. We may here observe, that the *Alexandrian* Copy distinguishes the *Sons of God*, Gen, vi. 2. which had to do with the wicked Daughters of *Cain*, before the Children of *Seth* had been perverted; from the *Sons of God*, or the Children of *Seth*, v.4. with whose Wives, of the Posterity of *Cain*, those *Sons of God* had also to do after their Perversion. Which Copy exactly agrees with all our Accounts oherbsf these two Sets of *Gigantick* Offspring before the Flood, Chap. Vi. 4. And this Distinction in *Moses*, between the *Angels of God*, and the *Sons of God*, seems to me, to be just; and to give the greatest Light to the present matter, of the Descent of the *Egregori*, and the Origin of the several Sorts of *Antediluvian Giants* from them.

(3.) This Account in *Enoch* is absolutely necessary for the Solution of that otherwise insoluble Problem, of the vast Bulk of many *Antediluvian*, and of certain *Postdiluvian Giants*: which yet is fully attested to by all ancient Records whatsoever. I do not mean here such smaller and later *Giants*, as *Goliath*, of the Height of four, or five, or perhaps at the utmost, of six Cubits: which is by no means incredible in the present State of things, especially nearer those Ages, when all the ancient Measures taken from human Bodies show that those Bodies in general were one eighth, if not one seventh taller than they now are; but I mean such *Giants* as were seven, or nine, or twelve: for so far go the sacred

See Gen. vi. 4 Bar. iii.26. Testament of Jud. §.3. Sanchoni-atho, in the Append. To the Ess. On the O.T. p.170 Grot. De. Veritat. Relig. Christ. L.L. §. 16. Huet.

13

Accounts of the Jews; or even twenty four, or thirty three, or 60 Cubits tall: for so far go the direct Heathen Testimonies in this Matter; to say nothing of the still greater Measures of the Poet's. Now to suppose, that the bare Intermarriages of the Sons of *Seth*, with the Daughters of *Cain*; i.e. of the Worshippers of the true God with *Idolaters*; should produce such enormous *Giants*, is contrary to all Fact and Experience: which shows that such gigantick Stature of Children has no Dependance on the Virtues or Vices of Parents. But that unnatural or monstrous Mixtures may produce an unnatural or monstrous Offspring; and that what Men weakly call the bare *Imagination* of the Mother, *not knowing*, in the meantime, *what they say, nor whereof they affirm*, may greatly affect the Child, is very agreeable thereto. So that this Account in *Enoch*, I only mean as explained in the Testament of *Reuben*, gives us such a rational Cause of this enormous Stature of the old *Giants* as we otherwise are utterly at a Loss for: and is therefore so far from rendering this Book incredible, as is commonly supposed; that it is a strong Attestation to its genuine Truth and Antiquity. Nor does *Enoch* and *Moses* give any other Account of the *Origin* of that great Wickedness which brought on the Deluge; I mean, as derived from *antediluvian Giants*, than what *Ovid* had learned out of those ancient Heathen Records which he made use of, when he composed the first Book of his *Metamorphoses*: which must have been primarily derived from this book of *Enoch*; the only antediluvian Record

Quest. Alnetan. L. II. 12. No. 3 || Vid. Lamy. De Tabernac. & Templ. I.8.

Enoch §. I-5 Test. of Reub. §. 5.

Ovid Metamorph. L. I.

that came among the Greeks or Latins of those Ages.

Vers. 151-315.

If any wonder at my mention of certain *postdiluvian Giants* also, whose vast Bulk ought to be accounted for in the Manner here described; he is to Observe, that we have a like Relation, out of the Revelation of *Moses*; to be hereafter set down; of the Descent of the *Giants*, the Offspring of the *Egregori*, 340 Years after the Flood; who seem to have introduced that Idolatry and Wickedness into the new World, Which had been washed away with the old one itself, at the Deluge; of which more hereafter. Nor do the Records which *Ovid* followed at all disagree with this part of our Account, but confirm it also. And to the like unnatural Mixtures of these *postdiluvian Giants*, the Offspring of the *Egregori*, with Women, do I ascribe those Races of enormous *Giants* after the Flood. And these, as we find by the Writings of *Moses*, lasted till the Introduction of the *Israelites* into the Land of *Canaan*: when *Og*, the King of *Bashan*, who reigned at, or near Mount *Hermon* (the very place of the Descent of the antediluvian *Egregori*; as we shall find presently;) had a *Bed 9 Cubits long, and 4 Cubits broad*. By whose Death an end was put to the Race of these *postdiluvian Giants*; as *Moses* also informs us.

Meta-morph. I.v. 416. &c.

Numb. Xiii:28-32, 53. Deut. Ii.10, II. 20,21. iii. 8-13. ix,2.

Deut. iii. II.

(4.) This Account in *Enoch* is also necessary for the Solution of another Problem, otherwise equally insoluble: I mean the true Origin of *Judicial Astrology*, and of all the several Species of *Magick-Art* with all those Charms or Incantations, † poisonous Herbs, Love-potions, Ceremonies, and Fopperies, depending on

† *See Test. Jos. §.6.*

them, or taught with them, so famous in all Antiquity; and by which so great a part of Mankind have always been, and still are deluded, and entangled in the grossest *Idolatry* and *Superstition*. Now of this whole Matter, *Enoch* gives us a most just and natural Account: entirely agreeing with the old and new *Testament*, and with all the primitive Books of *Judaism*, and *Christianity*; I mean, by assuring us, that they were derived from the same wicked and unclean Spirits, which had themselves fallen from their Obedience to their Creator, and who descended to the Earth from the lowest Region of our Air, where they lived in the immediate Neighbourhood of Mankind. So that this book of *Enoch*, by giving us such a rational Account of the Origin of all these wicked Arts, as we are otherwise utterly at a Loss for; is so far from rendering the Record before us incredible, as is commonly supposed; that it is, rather an Attestation to its genuine Truth and Antiquity.

Enoch. §. 2. 5.

(5.) There are several standing Monuments and Memorials of certain Facts related in this book of *Enoch*, still remaining, as Evidences of the Truth of those Facts. Thus the Memory of the *Descent* of these *Egregori*, and that in the Days of *Jared*, and that on a Mountain, by the Springs of *Jordan*, or, as the *Hebrews* write it, *Jarden*, which signifies and is preserved by the Name of the principal River of *Palestine* to this Day. Nor have we any other probable Derivation of it. Thus, the Memory of the same Descent of the *Egregori*, upon the Mountain *Hermon*, is preserved by that Name, which denotes that *Anathema*, or Curse, or Adjuration, by which the *Egregori* conjured

Enoch §.I.

Vid. Orig. Tom. VIII, in Joan. p.132. Reland Palest. I. 43.

together in *Enoch*. Which Name *Hermon* continues to belong to the same Mountain, to this Day. Nor have we any other probable Derivation of it. Thus also *Sanchoniatho*, the *Phoenician* Antiquary, describes the same earliest *Giants* before the Flood, as living and taking their Names from Mount *Cassius, Libanus, Antilibanus,* and *Brathys,* on which they seized: two of which, at least, are very near to Mount *Hermon*; on which *Enoch* says the *Egregori* descended: and both retain the Names of their several *Giants* to this Day. Nor have we any other certain Derivation of them. Thus, lastly, that Divine Denunciation or Curse upon Mount *Hermon* in *Enoch*, 'that Cold, and Snow, and Frost should never depart from it nor should Dew descend upon it, unless it were for a Curse, until the Day of Judgment', Appears to have been since fulfilled, by the Testimony of *Jerom* himself, an Inhabitant of *Palestine*; who assures us, that it was usual, in his Days, 'to carry Snow in Summer from this Mountain, [*over all the Mountains of* Libanus *and* Antilibanus] as far as Tyre itself'. The *Samaritan* Interpreter also, with the *Jerusalem Targum*, both call this Mountain, by way of eminence, the *Mountain of Snow. Eusebius* also, and *Jerom*, and *Hilary*, all agree, that in their Days the Gentile *Idolaters* had a famous Temple, by the same Mountain, for the Exercise of their profane Religion there: and by that means, as Hilary says, they bear witness to the Propriety of the Name *Anathema*, given to it in the Book before us. And whether the *Druses*, that are said to this Day, to act the greatest Lewdness, and to deny the Resurrection and to worship the Devil

Enoch §. I.

Reland. Palest. I. 49. Append to Ess. on the O.T. p.170

Enoch §.I0.

See Reland. Palest. p. 323, 324.

[*Baal Hermon. Judg. III.3.*]

instead of God, in Mount *Libanus,* or nor far from this Mount *Hermon,* be not the Remains of these Idolatrous and profane Worshippers will deserve to be considered. *See Hyde de Relig. vet. Perf. p.* 36, 491, 492, 493, 549, 554. Thus far of the *internal Characters;* which, for so small Fragments, are not a few, nor inconsiderable: I now proceed to the *external Testimonies.*

(6.) The Testaments of the XII *Patriarchs,* which, as we shall see anon, are themselves cited almost five Centuries before the Days of our Saviour, do fully, and frequently cite these Remains of *Enoch;* and that by *the Character the Scripture of Enoch: the Book of Enoch the righteous: the Scripture of Enoch: the Books of Enoch the righteous: the Scripture of the Law of Enoch: the Scripture or holy Scripture of Enoch: the Words of Enoch the righteous:* nor are the Things for which they cite them, at all unworthy of the highest of those Characters.

Test. Reu. §.5.
Sim. §.5.
Levi, §.10. 14. 16.
Jud. §.1.
Zab. §.3.
San. §.5.
Nept. §.4.
Benj. §.9.

(7.) *Alexander Polyhistor,* a learned Heathen, that wrote about a Century before the Christian *Era* assures us, that *Eupolemus,* another learned Heathen, somewhat elder than himself, wrote about *Enoch,* in these Words: 'It was *Enoch* who was the Inventor of Astrology [Astronomy,] and not the *Egyptians'* --- 'That the *Greeks* said, *Atlas* was the Inventor of Astrology and that *Atlas* was the very same Person with *Enoch;* the Father of *Mathusalem,* and learned all of the Angels of God'. Now, as Dr. *Grabe* well observes, it appears, that *Eupolemus* was taught this Origin of Astronomy out of the book of *Enoch* before us, by *Syncellus'* Citation of these Words, then extant therein, and already set down: 'In the

Ap. Euseb.. Prep. IX. 17.

Spicileg.

165th Year of the Age of *Enoch*, and the 1286th from the Creation of the World, *Uriel*, the Archangel, who was set over the Stars, did, by the command of Almighty God, reveal to *Enoch* what made a Month; which was the place of the Tropick; and what made a Year; as we find it in *Enoch's* own Book. 'And that the Year contains 52 Weeks: and that 1286 Years contain 469390 Days, and 67056 Weeks: wherein neither the Month, nor the Tropick, nor the Years, nor their Measures were known by Mankind'.

Sec. I. Not. p. 345.

N.B. Since it is very probable, that the Tribe of *Nephtali*, who, in the Days of *David*, are said to have *had Understanding of the times, to know what Israel ought to do*, had so much Knowledge of the Months, the Tropicks, and the Years, as to determine the feasts and Fasts belonging to the several Months of the Year, in the Jewish Calendar, and this long before any Astronomy was known by the rest of their neighbouring Nations: it will be reasonable to suppose, that those *Nephtalites* who computed, nay, that *Moses* himself who ordained those feasts and Fasts and even *Abraham* himself, who is said to have taught such Parts of Astronomy long before him, learned the same from these original Accounts of *Enoch*; at least from such later Accounts as were taken from the former, and accommodated to the State of the Year, Month, and Calendar after the Deluge.

I Chr. xii. 32.

Vid. Eupol. ap. Euseb. Prep. IX. 17. Joseph. Antiq. VII. 8.

N. B. The Numbers in *Syncellus*, from his Copies of the book of *Enoch*, and of other Apocryphal Fragments, are derived from that Chronology which the common Copies of the *Septuagint* Version contain, as to the Interval before the Flood: and suppose the Solar Year to have 365 Days, without the quarter of a Day: (the *Chaldean* Year in *Ptolemy*'s Canon.) Though whether these Numbers be *Enoch*'s, or the other's own Numbers: or whether they have not been fitted to the *Septuagint* Chronology, since that Version and Chronology were admitted by the Hellenist Jews, and by the Christians, will deserve to be considered: Specially, since a very different Chronology of that Interval is afforded us by all the other original Records that we have; I mean by the *Hebrew*, the *Samaritan*, and *Josephus*. See *the Ess. on the O. T. p.* 22. 205.

(8.) When St. *Paul* enjoins Christian Women, to have a *Veil* for the covering of their *Head, because of the Angels, Tertullian*'s Interpretation, approved of by our very learned Dr. *Davies*, is much the most probable, that the Apostle meant this caution to be necessary, because Women, in the Words of *Reuben, did deceive the* Egregori [or fallen *Angels*] *before the flood when by seeing those Women continually, they desired one the other*. And if this be the true Interpretation, tis probable, that St. *Paul* owned the Truth, and genuine Antiquity of this book of *Enoch*; from which originally that History was derived.

I Cor. xi 10.

In Epit. Lactant. C. 21.

Test. Reub. §.5.

(9.) When St. *Peter* affirms, *that God spared, not the Angels that sinned, but cast them down to Hades, and delivered them into Chains of Darkness, to be reserved unto Judgment*; or, in the Words of St. *Jude*, upon the very same Occasion, that, The *Angels which kept not their first Estate, but left their own Habitation, God hath reserved into everlasting Chains, under Darkness, unto the Judgment of the great Day*; there is little reason to doubt, but both of them directly refer to certain known Parts of our *Enoch*: especially when the following Words in *Jude*, do so plainly relate to the same History. *Sodom and Gomorrha, and the Cities about them were guilty of Uncleanness, after the like manner with the fallen Angels*, mentioned in the Verse before; and went after strange Flesh, or made unnatural Mixtures as they did. And if this be the true Interpretation, both St. *Peter* and St. *Jude* must also probably have owned the Truth and genuine Antiquity of this book of *Enoch*. Nor will it be any wonder, that St. *Paul* and St. *Peter* should be supposed to cite this Book, when it is so undeniable, that St. *Jude* does: as will appear under the next Argument.

Jud. v. 6.

Enoch §.6. v. 7

See Ess. on the O.T. p.313, 314, 315.

(10.) St. *Jude* is express for the Authority, the Prophetick Authority of our *Enoch*, and his being that very *Enoch* who lived before the Flood, and was translated into Heaven. His Words are these, Enoch *also, the seventh from* Adam, *prophesied of these, saying; Behold, the Lord cometh with ten thousands of his Holy Ones, to execute Judgment upon all, and to convince all that are ungodly among them, of all their ungodly Deeds, which they have ungodlily committed, and of all the hard Speeches which ungodly Sinners have spoken against him*. This Testimony is too plain to need a Comment. Nor is it reasonable to object, that neither this, nor the other, famous Prophesies quoted out of *Enoch*, in the Testament of the XII *Patriarchs*, are now found in those Parts of *Enoch* which are preserved; since, by the old *Stichometria*; to be hereafter set down in Part: *Enoch* had 1500 ςιχοι, and that about three quarters of that Book, at least, are lost: and since

v. 14, 15.

21

very little of what is preserved belongs to any other of *Enoch*'s Treatises, but what concerned the *Egregori* in his first Book.

(11.) To say nothing of *Philo*, who read Gen. vi. 4. *The Angels of God saw the Daughters of Men*, with our *Alexandrian* Copy; and so confirms the Foundation of *Enoch*'s Account concerning the *Egregori*: *Josephus* himself, not only agrees with *Philo* in the Reading or Interpretation of that Text of *Moses*, and so confirms the Foundation of *Enoch*'s Account of the *Egregori* also; but by making mention of the great Corruption of the World, as brought on in the seventh Generation from *Adam*; i.e. in the Days of *Enoch*; of Astronomy, as derived from the Antediluvians; and of Noah, as a Preacher of Repentance, may seem to have seen, and followed this book of *Enoch*. Yet because *Josephus* usually confines himself to the *Hebrew Canon* while *Enoch* seems always to have been a Part of the *Apocrypha*, I cannot speak with any Assurance of this Testimony of *Josephus*.

Phil. de Gygant.

Joseph. Antiq. I.3.

(12.) The Author of. the *Recognitions*, who is the only very ancient Christian that has been supposed to agree with the Moderns; in expounding the Intercourse of the *Sons of God*, or *Angels of God*, with the *Daughters of Men* in *Moses*, as if it only concerned Men of an *Angelick Character*, does yet give us this Account of the Origin of Idolatry and of Art-Magick; 'Certain Angels, *says he*, left that course of Life which belonged to their proper Order, and began to favour the Vices of Men, and after a sort to offer their Assistance, in an unworthy Manner, to their Lust; that so, by their means, they might the

Recog. IV.26.

I.29

better be subservient to their own Pleasures. Now these Angels, that they might not seem to be inclined of their own accord, to submit to such an unworthy Ministration, taught Men, that *Demons* might be made obedient to Men by certain Arts; i.e. by magical Invocations. Accordingly, They filled the whole World hence, as out of a Furnace, or a Shop, with the Smoke of Impiety, and took away the Light of Piety from it'. Which Account is plainly derived from this book of *Enoch* originally; and entirely supposes the authentick Nature, and genuine Antiquity of it. *IV. 30.*

(13.) *Irenaeus* says, 'that *Enoch* pleased God without Circumcision: and though he was but a Man, yet was he an Ambassador to the Angels; and was translated, and is preserved to this Days, as a witness of the Judgment of God: that when the Angels, upon their Transgression, fell down to the Earth, for a Judgment upon them; a Man that pleased him was translated unto Salvation'. Which Passage seems to be derived, in part, from this book of *Enoch*: and, so far to confirm its just Antiquity and Authority. *IV. 30.*

(14.) *Clement* of *Alexandria* 'believed, that certain of the Angels fell down from Heaven, out of the love of Women'. And he taught, 'that those Angels, whose Lot was above, condescended to Pleasures, [of another Nature,] and told Secrets to Women, and whatever had come to their Knowledge: while the rest of the Angels concealed the same, or rather reserved these things to the coming of the Lord: and that from thence did flow the Doctrine of Providence, and Revelation of sublime Things'. *Pedag. III.2.* *Strom. V. p.550.*

He also elsewhere, cites *Daniel* and *Enoch* as declaring much the same elevated Philosophick Notions: and particularly he affirms, that *Enoch* said, the Angels that were Transgressors taught Men Astronomy, [Astrology:] and Divination, and the other Arts'. So that *Clement* seems to have had no doubt as to the genuine Truth and Antiquity of this Book, out of which all these Passages are evidently taken.

Eclog. p. 801.

p.808

(15.) *Tertullian* affirms, "that *Enoch* of old, predicted, that the *Demons*, and the *Spirits* of forsaken Angels would convert all the Elements, every Part of the World's Furniture, that is contained either in Heaven, in the Sea, or in the Earth unto Idolatry; that they might be consecrated in the Place of God, in Opposition to the Lord. — That he condemned before hand, at once the Worshippers of an Idol, and they that make it; that the Holy Spirit foreseeing, from the beginning, that even the Doors would be turned into Superstition, foretold the same by his most ancient Prophet *Enoch*: that the same Angels who discovered such Matters, and such Enticements, viz. what belongs to Ornaments of Gold, and precious Stones, and the Ways of preparing them; and, who, among other things, taught how to beautify the Eye-lids, and to die Fleeces of Wool, were Condemned of God; as *Enoch* relates, &c. 'that he knows indeed that some '*Persons* did not admit of the *Scripture. of Enoch*, because it was not admitted into the Canon of the Jews, &c, But, however, since *Enoch* did, in the same Scripture, foretell things that concerned the Lord, nothing at all ought to be rejected by us, in which we are concerned. That

De Idol. §.4.

§.15. See Zeph. I. 9.

De Cult. Fem. L. II. §.10. Vid. L. I. §. 2.

L.I. §.3.

we read farther, that *all Scripture*, that may edify us, *is given by Divine Inspiration*: that it may well be supposed, that this *Scripture* is rejected, by the Jews, on the same Account, that they reject other Books of the like Nature because they *resound Christ*: that 'tis no manner of wonder, that while the Jews would not receive Him, when he was speaking to them Face to Face, they should not receive certain Scriptures which spake of him; and that the Testimony of *Jude* the Apostle afforded additional Strength to *Enoch'*. So that *Tertullian* was not only a Believer in this Scripture of *Enoch*, but a zealous Vindicator of its sacred Authority also.

N.B. *Tertullian* here intimates, very justly and shrewdly, that the principal Reasons of any doubt about the Authority of this book of *Enoch*, and others of a like nature, in the Christian Church, was from its absence from the Jewish Canon; and the Ill-will the Jews bare to Jesus Christ, who was therein most plainly described: as the Passages referred to in the Testaments of the XII *Patriarchs* do also demonstrate. Neither of which ought to be of any weight with us. Especially, since it appears to have been a most ancient Book, belonging to the Jewish Nation alone, and by that alone to have been delivered to the first Gentile Christians. Nor is it to be at all wondered at, that when the Jews had crucified Jesus of *Nazareth*, they should endeavour to set aside the Authority of any such Books as this of *Enoch*, and that of the Testaments of the XII Patriarchs, which so strongly, and undeniably, demonstrated his being no other than their true Messiah.

(16.) *Origen* himself, though he were persuaded by those Jews that taught him the *Hebrew* Language, to have as mean an Opinion as possible of all such Books, as too plainly supported the Christian Religion against them, yet does he several times cite this book of *Enoch* by Name as laying claim to a Prophetick Character; as having an excellent Passage like one in *Hermas*; as containing many secret and recondite Notions concerning the Stars; and as owned by some for little or nothing inferior to the *Divine Books* themselves: although he did not himself care to lay any Stress on its Authority, because the Jews of his Age did not admit it into their *Hebrew* Canon.

(17.) The most learned and accurate Author of the *Synopsis Sacra Scriptura* an *Alexandrian* that had no Correspondence with the *Hebrew* Jews, and so was not biased by their Authority; and one that was nearly contemporary with *Origen*; as will hereafter appear; is so far from any Suspicion about the Antiquity and Authority of this Book, or of the Testaments of the XII *Patriarchs*, that though he knew they were neither in the Jewish *Hebrew* Canon, nor were publickly read in the Christian Churches, yet does he put them at the Head of the *Sacred Apocrypha*, or *concealed Books of the Old Testament*.

(18.) *Anatolius* of *Alexandria* a learned Christian Chronologer, little later than the two former, directly cites τα μαθηαματα; the *Mathematicks*, of the same book of *Enoch*, as authentick Evidence to prove, that the Jews first Month [*Nisan*] was about the [*Vernal*] Equinox. Which Passage well agrees to my former

26

Conjecture, that the Jews originally derived their VII. p. 187. Astronomy from the book of *Enoch*, and regulated their Calendar therefrom in all the past Ages.

(19) *Cyprian* affirms, that 'they were fallen and apostate Angels that shewed the use of precious Ear-rings, and all the rest of the superfluous Ornaments of Women, among the rest of their Arts; when they descended to earthly Pollutions, and left their heavenly Vigour: that they were De Hab. these Angels that taught Women to make their Virg. p. 71. Eyes black, and to paint their Faces red, and to change the natural Colour of their Hair, and to adulterate their Mouth and Head; and all this, at the same time, when they lost their Chastity to them'. Which whole Account is evidently taken out of this Book of *Enoch*. So that there is no doubt but *Cyprian* believed the Truth and Authority of the same book of *Enoch*.

(20.) That the Jews have not always rejected this Book of *Enoch*, appears by the Citations made out of it, as out of a genuine sacred Book, by some of them, even as early as the Book *Zohar*. Thus *Manahem*, a *Rabbi* of the thirteenth Century, assures us, that *Enoch* said, I saw in *Paradise* the great Angels of the Ministry, and they cried *Holy, Holy, Holy,* &c. As also, that See Grabe certain of the latter *Cabbalists* said, that they Spicileg. Sec. I. Not. found in the book of *Enoch*, the Son of *Jared*, that p.355. a certain Secret was revealed to him, when God Fabric. took him away, together with the rest of his Pseudepig. V. T.p. wonderful Secrets. Moreover, says he, there is 208,209. mention made of that Book by our *Rabbins* in *Zohar*. And know thou, says he, that according to the Words of that Book, the inferior *Paradise* was prepared from that Day wherein the Spirits of the Just were created, to dwell there in their own Figure. Thus also *Manasseh Ben Israel,* assures us, that they understood by the book of *Enoch,* that God, after he had taken *Enoch* up, and had shewed him all his Treasures, superior and inferior, he shewed him also the Tree of Life; and that Tree which he had forbidden *Adam* to eat of. And that he saw the place of *Adam* in *Paradise,* in which had *Adam* observed that Precept, he had lived for ever, and continued to all Eternity. But because he did not obey the Precept of his Lord, therefore was he cast out to his own Loss, and suffered Punishment. *Ludovicus Capellus* produces also another place out of the Book *Zohar,* where it speaks of the Fall of the Angels *Aza* and *Azael,* as also of the *Nephilim,* or old Giants: which must very probably have been taken out of the same book of *Enoch.* As does also *Sgambat* produce another, wherein he mentions. the same *Enoch.* All which Testimonies shew, that the ancient Jews, even as early as the Book *Zohar,* were not unacquainted with the Antiquity and Authority of this Book of, *Enoch;* and probably had some *Hebrew* Copy or Version of it among them.

(21.) *Athanasius,* in the Additions to the *Synopsis Sacra Scripture,* if they be his; and in his more undisputed Festal Epistle, is greatly concerned to run down many sacred Books, which till then had been of the highest Authority in the *Alexandrian* Church, and, indeed, in all *Christian* Churches, excepting perhaps those of *Judea*: and particularly is very angry at the Books then called *Apocrypha.* So that though he mention not himself either the book of *Enoch*, or the Testaments of the XII *Patriarchs*, yet is there little question but he was for rejecting them entirely. And from this *Athanasius*, as I take it, among the *Greeks* and his zealous Follower *Jerom*, among the *Latins*, it was, that these and many more ancient sacred Books, which till then were generally and justly of great Authority among *Christians*, were by Degrees discarded and not a few of them lost, for many generations. But what I here produce *Athanasius* for, is this; that he confesses there were some Christians, even as late as his Age, who valued as sacred, those *Apocryphal* Books: and for this additional Observation, which I must make upon this Occasion, that However, the Jews had formerly prevailed upon some of the primitive Christians to *doubt* about this book of *Enoch*, and the other Books called *Apocrypha*, yet could they never prevail with any hitherto properly to deny or *reject* any one of them. That was peculiar to the *Athanasians*: and *Athanasius* himself appears to have been the very first Christian that ever did entirely deny or reject them. The Reason of which Boldness will readily appear when we come to treat of the *Synopsis Sacra Scriptura*, and of *Athanasius*'s bitter Opposition thereto hereafter.

(22.) *Hilary* of Poitiers says, That this *Hermon* is a Mountain in *Phoenicia*, whose Interpretation is *Anathema*. For what the *Latins* call *Anathema*, in the Hebrew is *Hermon*; that there is a thing related in he knew not whose Book, [*the Book of* Enoch,] that Angels desired the Daughters of Men, when they descended from Heaven; and

In Psalm

29

that they principally banded together upon this high Mountain. cxxxii. 3.

(23.) *Jerom* confesses, that *Jude*, the Brother of *James*, the Author of one of the seven Catholick Epistles, takes a Testimony out of this Apocryphal book of *Enoch*: nor does he deny but that the Testimony cited by St. *Jude* was then extant therein: as he elsewhere openly confesses, 'St. *Paul* took many other Citations out of Apocryphal Books also'. Yet does the same *Jerom* venture to condemn all those Books notwithstanding: because they did not appear in the *Hebrew* Canon of the Old Testament of that Age. Nay, if we believe him, to that Degree of Impudence had the *greatest Part* [he means, I suppose, only of the *Athanasians*] proceeded in his Days; that St. *Jude* himself, was, by that *greatest Part rejected*, because he so evidently quoted this Apocryphal book of *Enoch*. And if so, very, happy it was for St. *Paul*, and for us, that He escaped the like Rejection by the same majority: since *Jerom* confesses, that St. *Paul* took *many* Citations out of the Apocryphal Books; while he alleges but one that St. *Jude* had taken from them. However, *Jerom* himself soon contradicts what he had said about the Rejection of *Jude* on account of this Quotation by the *Majority*: since he immediately adds, that, 'However, this Epistle of *Jude* had then obtained Authority by its Antiquity, and long life, [in the Church,] and was still computed among the Books or holy Scripture'. Nor, indeed, is there any one Canon or Catalogue of the Books of the New Testament, either earlier or later than *Jerom*, so far as I have observed, that have fewer

Catal.
Scrip. Eccl.
In Jude

In Tit. I.

Catalog.
Script.

than seven Catholick or Canonical Epistles, or that omit this of *Jude* among them; as will appear hereafter. However, this Confession of *Jerom*'s, that after all, St. *Jude*'s Epistle, which had most openly cited *Enoch* as a true Prophet, before the Flood, and as having an eminent Prophecy still preserved, was, till his very Days, esteemed by the Church, one of the seven *Catholick* or *Canonical Epistles*, and a Book of *Holy Scripture* is no small Attestation to its genuine Antiquity, and to that sacred Authority, which it had anciently among Christians. *Eccles. In Jude*

(24.) The Author of that Commentary on the Psalms, which is extant among the Works of *Jerom*, but appears rather to be a Collection out of him, and many other Expositors, mentions this book of *Enoch* as one of the Apocryphal Books, that was then very well known in the Church, and spoken of by the elder Expositors. He confesses also, that Origen had cited it, for the Confirmation of somewhat that he esteemed Heretical. *In Psal. cxxxii 3.*

(25.) *Augustin*, who followed his *Athanasian* Leaders, and was willing to 'get clear of this, and other Books called *Apocrypha*', does yet confess, that so far of this of *Enoch*, as is approved of, and alleged by St. *Jude*, must be authentick, and contains *Divine Sentiments*. He also intimates, that it was the *very great Antiquity* of this, and the like Books, that gave the Jews and Christians room to suspect or reject them. Which Concession strongly confirms their genuine Antiquity and Authority. It being certain, as has been already observed, that if this Book had such great Antiquity, nay, if it was written at all *De Civitat Dei. XV. 23. XVIII.38.*

before the coming of Christ, or even before the Destruction of *Jerusalem* by *Titus*, it must be genuine.

(26.) *Zosimus Panopolites*, as *Syncellus* informs us, Observes, that the *holy Scriptures*, or holy *Books* say, 'that there is a certain Species of *Demons*, that make use of Women', that *Hermes* *p. 270. prius.* also makes mention of this, in his Physicks; and that almost all Writings, both open and apocryphal, make mention of it. This therefore is that which the ancient and *divine Scriptures* say, *p. 13. Fabric. P.183, 184.* 'that Angels lusted after Women, and came down, and taught them all the Works of Nature. For which cause, when they had offended, they 'continued excluded out of Heaven; because they had taught Men all things that were wicked, and did no way profit the Soul. The same Scriptures say, that of them were begotten the *Giants*'. All which Account is evidently in Confirmation of *Enoch*, as a Part of the *holy*, *ancient*, and *divine Scriptures* of the Old Testament.

(27.) *Georgius Syncellus*, when he wrote his Chronography, about A. D. 790, speaks often of this book of *Enoch*; but, like a true *Athanasian*, is very angry at it, and at other such Books, which had been long rejected by the *Athanasians* though without the least Pretense of any real Evidence for such their Rejection, He only say, 'that *Enoch* was an Apocryphal Book, and in some things of Uncertain Authority'. However, since almost all that we have left us of this most ancient Record, is owing to this Author's Extracts out of him, it is not fit to omit him. And pity, great pity it is, that *Syncellus* ventured to transcribe no more: seeing the Book itself, which was so common, and well known for eight or nine Centuries, has never been yet found, since the Revival of Learning among us.*p. 24.*

(28.) In the Stichometria of *Nicephorus, Patriarch* of *Constantinople*, about A. D. 800; to be hereafter set down in part: *Enoch* and the [XII] *Patriarchs*, are at the Head of the sacred Apocryphal Books of the Old Testament, as the Author of the *Synopsis* had long before placed them: and the Number of the ςιχοι, or Verses, in the *Greek*, are 4800; and in the old Version only 1500, or not quite a third Part so large as the Testament of the XII *Patriarchs*; which in the same Stichometria has in the Greek 5100; and in the Latin, 4800 Verses.

(29.) In another Index of the sacred Books published by *Cotelerius*; to be also hereafter set down in part: *Enoch* and the [XII] *Patriarchs* stand in the second and fourth Places of the same sacred Apocryphal Books of the Old Testament. And now the plain Result of all the foregoing Evidence is this, that before, and in the first Century, this book of *Enoch*, was, by all, owned to be genuine, to be a great *Apocryphal* or *Concealed* Treasure, nay, perhaps, the *oldest sacred Record* among Mankind; that the Apostles and Companions of the Apostles believed it to be so; that the first Gentile Christians received it from the Jews as such, and believed and quoted it as such, without Hesitation; till the unbelieving *Hebrew* Jews, finding the Strength of the Evidence therein contained for Christianity, gradually diminished its Reputation, and, at length, persuaded the Christians first to doubt of it, and then to reject it: which Rejection yet they could never entirely encompass, till *Athanasius* and his Followers resolved to lay aside this, and all the other Apocryphal Books of the Old and New Testament.

N. B. As to the ωλδυες το οpano *The Tables of Heaven*, sometimes quoted in the Testaments of the XII *Patriarchs*, and the Prayer of *Joseph*; which are, by Mr. Dodwell, supposed to belong to this *Book of Enoch*, and about which he has made a particular, Dissertation, I see no Foundation for all those learned Disquisitions about them. They seem to me to mean only this, that, as usually, the Prophets *heard Words* spoken to them, in the Visions they received; so did they sometimes *read* such *Words* represented as *written upon Tables* before their Eyes: and since these Tables in the Visions, were supposed to be seen *in Heaven*, they are fitly called *The Tables of Heaven*. Nor do I at all apprehend any farther Mystery in this Matter.

Test. Levi, §.5.
Test. Nep. §.5.
Test. Aser §.7.
Prayer of Joseph Ap. Grabe, Spicileg. Sec.I Not. p. 338-343. Et Fabric. P. 551-559

Introduction to the 21st-Century Edition of
Testaments of the 12 Patriarchs
by William Whiston.

It may surprise modern readers that the *Testaments of the Twelve Patriarchs* is one of four books which centuries ago were included in Armenian Orthodox Bibles.

These books are, *Joseph and Aseneth, Lives of the Prophets, 3 Esdras, and the Testaments of the Twelve Patriarchs*. Also, there exists ancient record that *The Book of Enoch* at one time was also included in the Bibles of Armenian Orthodoxy, although no copy of *Enoch* now exists in the Armenian language.

The *Testaments* is important as it bears ancient witness to the *Book of Enoch* being treated as a book of holy Scripture by each of the twelve sons of Jacob.

THE

TESTAMENTS

OF THE

XII *PATRIARCHS,*

the Sons of *Jacob,*

Delivered to their Sons.

The Testament of R E U B E N.

A copy of the Testament of *Reuben,* concerning what he gave, in charge, to his Sons before he died; in the 125th year of his life. Two years after the decease of *Joseph,* his Sons, and his Sons Sons came to visit him in his sickness: And he said unto them, My Sons I die, and go the way of my fathers. And seeing there his brethren, *Judah, Gad,* and *Aser,* He said unto them, Lift me up my Brethren, that I may tell you, and my Sons, what I have hid in my heart: for I am from this moment drawing to my end. Then rising up he kissed them, and weeping said, Hearken, My Brethren; and you My Sons, give ear to your father *Reuben,* what I give in charge to you: Behold I charge you this day before the God of heaven, that ye walk not in the ignorance of youth and fornication; wherein I indulged myself, and *defiled the bed* of my father *Jacob.* For, I assure you, that the Lord did therefore strike me with a sore plague in my groin, for the space of seven months: and I had perished, if our father *Jacob* had not prayed to the Lord for me, because the Lord was minded to slay me. I was thirty years old when I did this evil in the sight of the Lord: and seven months was I sick to death, and with a free heart did I seven years penance before the Lord. *I drank no wine, nor strong drink: and no flesh came within my mouth, I tasted not any pleasant bread:* but I mourned for my Sin, because it was great: and there ought to be no such thing done in *Israel.*

Gen. xxxv. 22. xlix. 4.

Dan. x. 3.

§. **2.** And now, My Sons, Hear me, that. I may shew you what I saw concerning the seven Spirits of error in my repentance. *Beliar* sendeth seven Spirits against a man, which are the fountain of the works of youth: and seven Spirits are sent to man in his creation, whereby all his works are to be performed. The first is the Spirit of Life; wherewith is created his being. The second is the Spirit of Seeing; wherewith cometh desire. The third is the Spirit of Hearing; wherewith cometh learning. The fourth is the Spirit of Smelling; wherewith cometh a sensation for inspiration and expiration of the air. The fifth is the Spirit of Speech; wherewith knowledge is gained. The sixth is the Spirit of Tasting; wherewith comes the participation of meat and drink, and through

Vid. Herm. Mandat. 2. & Co- teler. Nat.

them is engendered strength: because the substance of strength is in meat. The seventh is the Spirit of Seed and Generation wherewith enters in sin, by pleasure. For this cause, that is the last thing of Creation, and the first of Youth: because it is full of ignorance and ignorance leadeth the younger sort as a blind man into a ditch; and as an Ox to a precipice.

§ 3. Besides all these, there is the eighth Spirit, which is that of Sleep: wherewith is created the wasting of nature, and the image of Death. With these Spirits, are mingled the Spirits of Error. Whereof, the first is the Spirit of Lechery; which lieth within the nature and senses of man. The second is the Spirit of Unsatiableness and lieth in the belly. The third is, the Spirit of Strife; and lieth in in the liver, and in the bile. The fourth is the Spirit of Bravery and Gallantness; that the party may appear comely to excess. The fifth is the Spirit of Pride; which moveth a man to mind great things, and to think highly of himself. The sixth is the Spirit of Lying or Vain-glory, in boasting falsely of a man's self; and in a desire to fill his talk, with accounts of his stock and kindred. The seventh is the Spirit of Unrighteousness, with theft, and violent grasping at others goods; in order to perform the lustful pleasures of the heart. For Unrighteousness worketh with all other Spirits, by taking guile for its partner. Unto all these Spirits, is matched the eighth Spirit; which is the Spirit of Sleep and Sluggishness, in error and imagination; and so the souls of all young folks perish, because their minds are darkened, and hidden from the truth, and understand not the law of God, neither obey the admonition of their fathers; as it befell me in my youth. And now, My Sons, Love the truth, and it shall preserve you: It is I that instruct you: Hearken to your father *Reuben*; and let not your eyes run a gazing after a woman; neither be ye alone with a woman that is married; neither do ye needlessly seek out what women are doing. For if I had not seen *Bilha* bathing her self, in a place that was covered, I had not fallen into that great wickedness. But my mind ran so upon the naked woman, that it suffered me not to sleep, till I had committed that abomination. For while our father *Jacob* was away at his father *Isaac*'s, and we were in *Gad*er, hard by *Ephrata*, a house of *Bethlehem*, *Bilha* was drunk; and as she lay asleep, uncovered in her chamber, I went in also, and seeing her nakedness wrought wickedness with her; and leaving her asleep went my way. By and by an Angel of God bewrayed my wickedness to my father *Jacob*; who coming home mourned for me; and touched not *Bilha* any more.

§. **4.** Do not you therefore look upon the beauty of women; neither muse you upon what they do: but walk with singleness of heart in the fear of the Lord; and busy your selves at your work, and in learning, and about your Flocks, until such time as the Lord shall give you such a yoke-fellow as it seemeth good to him: that you may not suffer as I have done. I had not the assurance to look *Jacob* in the face, or to speak to any of my Brethren till my father died; they did so much reproach me. And to this day my conscience pinches me on account of my Sin. Although my father bid me be of good cheer; for

Gen. xxxv. 21. Mic. iv.8.

that he had prayed to God for me, that the anger of the Lord might pass away from me; as the Lord shewed me. From that time therefore I kept myself, and did not Sin. On which account, My Sons, observe every thing that I give you in charge; and you shall not Sin. For fornication is the destruction of the Soul; it separates from God, and leads unto idolatry; for it seduces the mind, and the undemanding, and Brings young Men down to the grave before their time: for fornication hath destroyed many: for whether the party be old, or noble, it fixes a reproach upon him, with *Beliar*, and with the Sons of men. And it was because *Joseph* kept himself from all women, and cleansed his thoughts from every kind of uncleanness, that he found grace before the Lord, and before men. For the *Egyptian* woman did many things to him, and called to the *Magicians*, and brought to him a magick potion; but the purpose of his Soul did not admit an evil desire. Wherefore the God of my fathers delivered him from every visible and concealed kind of death. For In case fornication does not prevail over your mind, neither will *Beliar* prevail against you.

Test. Jos. §. 6.

§. 5. My Sons, women are wicked; because When they have no authority or power over a man, they contrive by their dress to draw him unto them; and him whom they cannot conquer by force, they conquer by deceit. For the Angel, of God said to me, concerning them, and taught me, that women are more subject to the spirit of fornication than men; and have contrivances, in their heart against men, and deceive them by their ornaments; and that in the first place they affect the mind, and by the Eyes sow poison; and then they carry them captive to the deed itself: for a woman cannot force a man. Avoid therefore, fornication, My Sons, and give it in charge to your Wives and Daughters, that they do not adorn their heads, and their faces: for every woman that deceives men by such arts, is reserved for the punishment of the future World. For so did they deceive the *Egregori*, before the Flood; when by seeing those women continually, they desired one the other; and they conceived in their mind what they would do, and they were transformed into the figures of men, and when their Husbands accompanied with them they appeared to them at the same time: and these women desiring their company, in their imaginations, bear *Giants*: for the *Egregori* appeared to them as reaching up to Heaven.

Enoch De Egreg. Jude. v. 6, 7.

§. 6. Keep your selves therefore from fornication, and if you will have a pure mind keep your senses from every female. Give the females also charge that they have no commerce with men; that they also may have a pure mind: for perpetual conversation, though the wicked act be not done, is to those females an incurable disease: but to you the eternal reproach of *Beliar*: for fornication hath neither understanding nor piety in it: and all violence of temper inhabits in the lust thereof. On this account ye will violently envy the Sons of *Levi*; and you will endeavour to be exalted above them; but will not be able. For God will execute vengeance for them, and ye shall die with an evil death. For God hath given to *Levi* the principality, and [next] to *Judah*. After him to Me, and to *Dan*, and to *Joseph* that we

Num. xvi. I.

should be rulers. On this account I charge you to hearken to *Levi*; for he shall know the Law of the Lord, and shall give distinct judgment, and [*ascertain the*] Sacrifices of all *Israel*, until the completion of the times of Christ, the High-Priest; of whom the Lord hath spoken. I adjure you by the God of Heaven, that you observe truth every one with his neighbour; and that you approach to *Levi* in humility of heart, that you may receive a Blessing from his mouth: for he shall bless *Israel* and [*approach ye also with humility of heart to*] *Judah*; for in him has the Lord chosen to reign over all the people. Do ye also worship his Seed: for He shall die for you in visible and invisible Wars, and shall be among you an eternal King.

§. 7. And *Reuben* died, when he had given [*this*] charge to his children: and they put him in a coffin; until they might bring him out of *Egypt*; when they buried him in *Hebron* in the double Cave, [*the Cave of Macpelah,*] where his Fathers *Gen. xxiii.* were.

S Y M E O N.

A Copy of the words of *Symeon* which he spake to his Sons, before he died, in the 120th year of his life: in which year *Joseph* died. They came to visit him in his sickness; and raising himself he sat up, and kissed them, and said unto them:

§. 2. Hearken, My Sons, hearken to *Symeon* your father; as to what I have in my heart. I was born the second Son of *Jacob* my father: and my mother *Lea* called me *Symeon*, because the Lord heard my prayer. I was very strong, I feared no *See &* labour, and was not afraid of any thing: for my *Correct.*

heart was hard, and my inward parts unmoved, and my bowels were without compassion: for courage is bestowed on men by the Most High, both as to Souls and Bodies. And at that time, I envied *Joseph*, because our father loved him; and I hardened my inward parts against him, to slay him: for the Prince of Error sent the Spirit of envy, and blinded my mind; so that I did not consider him as a brother, and had no regard to *Jacob* my father. But his God, and the God of his fathers, delivered him from mine hands. For as I went to *Shechem*, to carry ointment to the flocks; and as *Reuben* went to *Dothaim*, where lay our provisions, and all the treasure we had, *Judas*, my brother, sold him to the *Ishmaelites*. Now when *Reuben* came, he was grieved for he intended to preserve him for his father. But I was angry with *Judah*, that he let him go away alive: and I continued five months in my anger at him. However, the Lord hindered me, and did not permit me to lay hands upon him: for my right hand was half of it withered for seven Days: and I knew, My Sons, that this befell me for *Joseph*'s sake. Whereupon I repented, and wept, and prayed to the Lord, that he would restore my hand; and I would abstain from all pollution, and envy, and from all sort of folly: for I knew that I had intended to do what was wicked before the Lord, and before *Jacob* our father, out of envy to *Joseph* our brother.

§. 3. And now, My Sons, keep your selves from the Spirits of deceit and of envy; for envy has dominion of the entire mind of man, and does not suffer him either to eat or drink, or to do any thing that is good; it always suborns him

Gen. xxix. 35

Gen. xxxvii. 21, 22.

to slay him that is the object of envy, while He still flourishes, and the envious man withers away. I afflicted my Soul by fasting two years of days in the fear of the Lord: and I knew that the dissolution of envy is by the fear of God; if any one flies to the Lord, the wicked Spirit flies from him, and the mind becomes light. After which, the party sympathizes with him that is envied, He does not condemn those that love him, and so he ceases to envy any more.

§. 4. Now my father was still enquiring about me, because he saw me look sad; and, I said, I am not well inwardly: for I grieved more than all the rest, that I had been an occasion of the selling of *Joseph*. And when we went down into *Egypt*, and he bound me, I knew that I suffered justly, and I bare it patiently. Now *Joseph* was good man, and had the Spirit of God in him; he was of a compassionate and merciful disposition, and so he did not lay to heart what I had done to him: but he moreover loved me, as he also did his other brethren. Keep your selves therefore, My Sons, from all spite and envy; and go on in simplicity of Soul, and with a good heart; as mindful of your father's brother: [*Joseph:*] that God may give you grace and glory, and may send a blessing upon your Heads; as you see he did to him. All the while we lived with him, he never reproached us concerning that matter; but loved us as his own Soul: and bestowed honour upon us, more than upon his own Sons: and he freely bestowed upon us riches, and cattle, and the fruits of the land. Do you therefore, every one of you, My Dear Sons, love his brother with a good Heart, and banish away from you the Spirit

Gen. xlii. 24.

Test. Joseph §. 17.

44

of Envy: for that makes the Soul savage, and corrupts the Body suggests wrath and war to the Thoughts, and provokes Men to shed Blood, and puts the Mind into disorder, and suffers not the Understanding to exert it self: nay, moreover, it takes away Sleep, and brings disquiet upon the Mind, and trembling upon the Body: for even in Sleep, some spice of Malice remains in the Imagination, and gnaws the Man; it both disturbs his Soul, and disorders his Body, and awakes the Mind as out of a fright; and it appears to Men as what has a wicked Spirit, diffusing poison.

§. 5. It was for this reason, that *Joseph* was beautiful in his aspect, and fair in his countenance, because nothing that was wicked dwelt in him: for the countenance discovers when the Spirit is troubled. And now, My Sons, purify your Hearts before the Lord, and purify your ways before Men; and you shall find favour before God and Men. And keep your selves from fornication: for fornication is the mother of all evils: it is what separates us from God, and brings nigh to *Beliar*. For I saw in the character of the Scripture of *Enoch*, that your Sons, as well as your selves, will be corrupted by fornication, and will use their sword injuriously against *Levi*: but they will not be able to prevail against *Levi*: for he shall fight the battle of the Lord, and shall overcome all your encampment, and you shall become few in number; and be scattered in [*or by*] *Levi*, [*on account of your injury to* Levi.] *Judah*, shall be that tribe of you that shall afford you a Ruler; as our father *Jacob* also foretold, in his Blessings. [*Gen. xlix. 8——12.*]

Deut. xxxiii. 6. corrected. compare Numb. i. 25. with xxvi. 14.

§. 6. Behold, I have foretold you all things; that I may be clear of the sin of your Souls. But if you cast away from you envy, and all hardness of heart, my bones shall flourish as a rose in *Israel*; and my flesh as a lily in *Jacob*; and my odor, shall be as the odor of *Libanus*; [*frankincense*] and Holy ones, shall multiply out of me for ever; and their branches shall be for a long time: Then shall the seed of *Canaan* perish; and there shall be no remains of *Amalek*, and all the *Cappadocians*, [*Caphtorim*,] and all the *Hittites* shall be destroyed. Then shall the Land of Ham fail; and all [*her*] people shall perish. Then shall the whole Earth be at rest from trouble; and whatsoever is under the Heaven, shall be free from war Then shall *Sem* be glorified; because the Lord, the great God of *Israel* shall appear upon Earth, as a Man, and shall save *Adam* by Him. Then shall all the Spirits of Error be given to be trodden down; and Men shall reign over those wicked Spirits. Then shall I rise again with gladness, and shall bless the Most High for his wonderful works; when God shall take a Body, and shall converse with Men, and shall save them.

§. 7. And now, My Sons, Be obedient to *Levi*; and ye shall be redeemed by *Judah*. But do not ye exalt your selves in opposition to these two tribes: for out of them shall arise the Salvation of God. For the Lord will raise up out of *Levi** one that shall be as an High-Priest; and out of *Judah* one that shall be as a King; God and Man. So will he save all the Gentiles, and the flock of *Israel*. Wherefore I give you these things in charge, that you may give them in charge to your Sons, that they may observe them in their generations.

* *John the Baptist*

The Messiah

§. 8. And *Symeon* made an end of the charge that he gave to his Sons: and he slept with his fathers, being 120 years of age. And they put him in a coffin, made of wood that would not putrify; [*Shittim wood;*] in order to bring his * bones back to *Hebron.* And they brought them back in the *Egyptian* war privately: for the *Egyptians* kept the bones of *Joseph* in the private Sepulchres belonging to their Kings. For their Enchanters said to them, that when the bones of *Joseph* should be carried out of there would be a mist and darkness over all *Egypt*, and a very great plague upon the *Egyptians*; so that one man should not be able to find his brother, no not with a candle.

* A.M. 2863. In the latter of Ramses the Great, who conquered no small part of the then known World about that time. See my Chronological Table. Josephus perfectly agrees to this account of the Burial of the Patriarchs.

§. 9. And His Sons wept for *Symeon* their father, according to the custom of mourning. And they were in *Egypt* until the day when they went out of *Egypt* by the hand of *Moses.*

L E V I.

A copy of the words of *Levi*, what he gave in charge to his Sons, about all things that they were to do; and about all things that should befall them until the day of judgment. He was well in health when he called them to him, but he had a Vision that he should soon die. Now when they were gathered together he said to them,

See Mal. ii. 4, 5.

§. 2. I, *Levi* was conceived in *Charran*, and there was I born: and I afterward came with my father to *Shechem*. Now I was but young, about 20 years of age, when I, with *Symeon*, executed vengeance on upon account of, our sister *Dina*.

Gen. xxxiii 18. xxxiv 25, 26.

But as I was feeding the flock in *Abelmeholah*, The Spirit of Understanding of the Lord came upon me, and I saw that all men; had darkened their way, and that wickedness had built it self walls, and that iniquity sat upon towers: and I was grieved for mankind: and I prayed to the Lord that I might be saved. Whereupon sleep fell upon me, and I saw an high mountain; It was the *mountain of the field in Abelmebolah*: and, behold, the Heavens were opened, and an Angel of the Lord said to me, *Levi*, Come in hither: and I entered out of the first Heaven into the second: and there I saw water, hanging between this Heaven and that. And I saw a third Heaven, much more splendid than those two: for its altitude was immense. And I said to the Angel, Wherefore is this? And the Angel said to me, Do not thou wonder at these things: for thou shalt see four other Heavens, more splendid, and incomparably finer, when thou shalt ascend thither; [*to the third Heavens.*] For thou shalt stand near to the Lord, and shalt be his minister, and shalt declare his mysteries to men, and shalt openly foretell the future redemption of *Israel*: and by thee, and *Judah*, the Lord shall be seen among men, saving by them all mankind: and thy livelihood shall be out of the Lord's portion; and He shall be thy field, and vineyard, fruits, silver, and gold.

§. 3. Hear therefore what I have to say about the seven Heavens. The lowest is on that account the Most melancholy, because it adjoins to all the unrighteousness of Men. The second contains Fire, Snow, Hail, which are ready against the day when the Lord commands them, out of the righteous judgment of God. In this, are all the Avenging Spirits, made use of to bring vengeance on the unjust. In the third, are the Powers of the Hosts, [*Powers and Hosts,*] which are ordained against the day of judgment, to execute vengeance on the Spirits of Error, and of *Beliar*. But those which are unto the fourth [*Heaven*] above these, are Holy Ones: because the supreme Glory inhabits above all, in the Holy of Holies, above all Sanctity. In the next after this, are the Angels of the Presence of the Lord; who minister and make atonement with the Lord, for all the sins of Ignorance of the Righteous. Now these Offer to the Lord, as a sweet savour, a reasonable and unbloody Oblation. In the next under this, are those Angels, who carry answers to the Angels of the Presence of the Lord. In the next after this, are Thrones. and Authorities: wherein Hymns are offered to God perpetually. When therefore the Lord looks down upon us. We are all shaken; the Heavens also, and the Earth, and the Abysses are shaken at the Presence of his Majesty. But the Sons of Men still sin, and are insensible of these things, and provoke the Most High to anger.

Hab. iii. 6.

§. 4. Know ye therefore, that the Lord will execute judgment upon the Sons of Men, who, when the Rocks shall be rent, and the Sun be put out, and the Waters be dried up, and the Fire shall make a trembling, and the whole Creation shall be disordered, and the invisible Sprits shall melt away, and the invisible World shall be despoiled, at the passion of the Most High, will yet be incredulous, and continue in their unrighteous actions. For this reason shall they be adjudged to punishment. The Most High then has heard thy prayer, in order to separate thee from unrighteousness, and to make thee to him a Son, and a Servant, and a Minister of his Presence. Thou shalt be as a luminary to illuminate the posterity of *Jacob*, with the Light of Knowledge; and thou shalt be as a Sun to all the Seed of *Israel*; and a Blessing shall be given to thee, and to all thy Seed, until the Lord visit all the Gentiles in the bowels of his Son for ever. However, thy Sons will lay hands upon him to crucify him. And for this reason it is that Counsel and Understanding is given to thee, to admonish thy Sons about this Matter: for he that blesseth him shall be blessed: but those that curse him shall perish.

§. 5. And the Angel opened me the gates of Heaven, and I saw the Holy Temple, and the Most High upon the Throne of Glory. And He said to me, *Levi*, To thee have I given the blessings of the Priesthood, until I come and inhabit in the midst of *Israel*. Then the Angel conduced me down upon the Earth, and gave me a weapon, and a Sword; and said, Do thou execute vengeance on *Sychem*, for *Dina*; and I will be with thee: for the Lord hath sent me. And I slew at that time the Sons of *Emor*; as it was written in the *Tables of the Heavens*. And I said unto him, I beseech thee, O Lord, Tell me thy Name: that I may call upon thee in the day of affliction. And He said to me, I am that Angel who plead for the flock of *Israel*, that it may not be utterly smitten down: for every wicked Spirit sets himself against them. Now after this I awaked, and blessed the Most High, and that

Angel who pleaded for the flock of *Israel*, 'and all righteous Men.

§. **6.** And as soon as I came to my father, I found a brazen Shield: whence it was that the mountain was called... The *Shield*: for it is near *Gebal*, on the right hand of *Abila*: and I kept these words in my Heart. It was I that advised my father, and *Reuben* my brother, that he should declare to the Sons of *Emor* that they should be circumcised: for my zeal was kindled on account of that abomination they had wrought in *Israel*. I also slew *Sychem* among the first, and *Symeon* [*slew*] *Emor*. After which our brethren came and smote the City with the edge of the sword. Now our father heard of it, and was angry, and grieved because they had first received circumcision, and after that were slain: and he did otherwise in his blessings. For we sinned in that we did this without his approbation: and even he was afflicted in that day. But I saw that the Decree of God was for evil upon *Sychem*; because they would have done to *Sarah* as they did to *Dina* our sister; though the Lord hindered them. So also did they persecute *Abraham* our father, when he was a stranger; and they trampled on his flocks, when they were heavy upon him; as they did greatly torment *Jeblai*, one that was born in his house. Nay, indeed, they did the same thing to all strangers, seizing upon their wives by force, and driving those strangers into foreign countries. *And the wrath of the Lord came upon them to the uttermost.*

§. **7.** And I said to my father, Sir, Be not angry: for the Lord will bring to nought the *Canaanites* by thee, and will give their land to thee, and to

Gen. xxxiv 13, &c.

v. 25, &c.

v. 30.

xlix. 5, 6, 7.

Alluded to by St.Paul, I Thess. ii. 16.

Vid. Gen. xxxv. 5.

thy seed after thee: for from this day, shall the City *Sychem* be called, *The City of the foolish*: for as any one would deride a fool, so have we had them in derision; because they *wrought folly in Israel* in defiling our sister. Upon which we took our sister away thence; and removed and came to *Bethel*.

Gen. xxxiv. 31. xxxv. 1

§. 8. And here again, it was that I saw somewhat as I had done before; and this after we had stayed there 70 days. And I saw seven men in white raiment, who said to me, rise up, and put on the coat of Priesthood; the crown of Righteousness; the breastplate of Understanding; and the robe of Truth; and the [*golden*] plate of Faith; and the mitre of the Sign; and the ephod of Prophecy. And every one of them, brought his particular part of the Habit, and put them on me: and they said, From this time, be thou a Priest of the Lord, thou and thy Seed for ever. And the first of them, anointed me with Holy Oil, and gave me the Rod of Judgment. The second of them, washed me with pure water, and fed me with Bread and Wine, those Most Holy Things; and he clothed me with the holy and glorious Coat. The third, clothed me with a linen garment, which was like an Ephod. The fourth, put about me a Girdle, as it were of Purple. The fifth, gave me a branch of an Olive-Tree of fatness. The sixth, put a Crown upon my Head. The seventh, put a Mitre of Priesthood about my Head, and filled my hands with incense, that I might execute the office of Priesthood to the Lord. And they said to me, *Levi*, Thy seed shall be divided into three principal Branches, for a sign of the Glory of the

Lord who is to come. He that believeth, he shall be the first lot: and there shall not be any one greater than he. The second shall be in the Priesthood…. The third shall be called by a New Name; because a King shall be raised up out of *Judah* and shall ordain a New Priesthood, according to the type of the Gentiles, [*of Melchisedek*] and for all the Gentiles. Now his coming will be ineffable, as of a Prophet of the Most High, of the Seed of *Abraham* our father. Whatsoever is desirable in *Israel* shall be for thee, and for thy Seed; and ye shall eat every thing that is goodly to see to, and thy Seed shall distribute the table of the Lord; and out of them, shall be Priests and Judges and Scribes: for the Sanctuary shall be kept by their direction. And when I was awake, I understood that this [*vision*] was like the other. However, I kept this in my Heart, and did not declare it to any Man upon Earth.

§. 9. And after two days I and *Judah* went up to *Isaac*, with our father. And my Father's Father blessed me, according to the words of my visions which I had seen. And He would not go with us to *Bethel*. Now as we came to *Bethel*, my father *Jacob* saw in a vision concerning me, that I should be to them a Priest with God. And he rose up in the morning, and by me Offered tithes of all he had to the Lord. And we came to *Hebron* to dwell. And *Isaac* called me frequently to admonish me of the Law of the Lord; as the Angel of God had shewed me. And he instructed me in the Law of the Priesthood, of Sacrifices, of Burnt-offerings, of first Fruits, of Free- will-offerings, and of Thank-offerings.

Family of Eleazar. Family of Ithamar. Christian Priesthood.

Gen. xxxv. 1——15.

v. 27

And he spent some time every day in teaching me, and was diligent about me before the Lord. And He said to me, Preserve thy self, My Son, from the Spirit of Fornication: for it is a permanent evil, and will pollute thy Holy things by the means of thy Seed. Wherefore, take to thy self a wife, whilst thou art yet young, one that is without blot, unpolluted, but neither out of the race of Foreigners, nor of Gentiles. And before thou enter into the Holy place wash thy self all over; and when thou killest the Sacrifice wash thy self. And when thou gain preparest the Sacrifice wash thy Self. Bring before the Lord the fruit of 12 trees, that have their leaves continually; as *Abraham* instructed me; and Offer a Sacrifice of every clean Animal, and [ever}] clean Foul unto the Lord. Offer also the first fruits of what is first ripe, and of thy wine, a Sacrifice to the Lord: and every Sacrifice Shalt thou salt with salt. *Ezek. xlvii 7, 12. Apoc. XXII. 2.*

§. **10.** Now therefore, My Sons, keep whatsoever I give you in charge: for whatsoever I have heard of my father's I have declared to you. I am innocent of all your impiety and transgression, which you will be guilty of in the consummation of the ages, in dealing impiously with the *Saviour of the World*: seducing *Israel*, and stirring up great mischiefs to them from the Lord. And you will transgress, together with *Israel*; insomuch that *Jerusalem* will not be able to Support it self before the face of your wickedness. Nay, the veil of the Temple will be rent, and will not cover your shame. And you Shall be Scattered as Captives among the Gentiles; and you Shall be for a reproach and a *Gen. xviii. 19.*

curse, and for a conculcation: for the House which the Lord will choose, Shall be called *Jerusalem*: as is contained in the book of *Enoch* the righteous.

§. 11. When therefore I took me a wife, I was 28 years of age, and her name was *Melcha*, and she conceived and bare [*a Son,*] and called his name *Gersam*; because we were sojourners in our own land: for *Gersam* signifies a sojourner. And I knew this concerning him, that he would not be in the first rank. Moreover, *Kaath* was born in my 35th year, at Sun-rising. Now I saw in a Vision, that He stood in the midst of the Congregation on high. For which reason she called his name *Kaath*:.... which is [*a Congregation*;] [*the beginning of magnitude and instruction,*] A third Son she also bear to me, Merari, in the 40th year of my life; and because his mother had hard labour, she called him *Merari*, that is, *my bitterness*: for she died her self. Now *Jochabed* in the 64th year of my age was born in *Egypt*: for I was at that time glorious in the midst of my brethren.

§. 12. And *Gersam* took a wife, and she bear him *Lomni*, [*Lobni,*] and *Semei*. And the Sons of *Kaath* were *Abram*, [*Amram,*] *Isaar*, *Chebron*, and *Oziel*. And the Sons of *Merari* were *Molthe*, and *Omoise*. And in my 94th year *Abram*, [*Amram,*} took my daughter *Jochabed* to himself to wife; for they were born the same day, both He and my Daughter. I was 8 years old when I came into *Canaan*: and 18 years old when I slew *Sychem*: and 19 years old when I entered on the Priesthood: and at 28 years of age I took a wife: and when I was 40 [49] years old I entered into

Dele vel corrige.

Ex. vi. 16 &c.

Egypt. And behold now, My Sons, the third generation. *Joseph* died in my 118th year.

§. 13. And now, My Sons, I charge you, fear the Lord your God out of your whole Heart, and walk in simplicity of Heart, according to his whole Law. Do you also instruct your children in learning, that they may have Understanding in their whole Life, by reading continually the Law of God: for every one that shall know the Law of God shall be honoured, and shall nor be a stranger wherever he goes. For he shall have many friends more than his Parents had; and many Men shall desire to serve him, and to hear the Law out of his mouth. Exercise Righteousness, My Sons, upon Earth, that you may find it in the Heavens: and sow good things in your Souls, that you may find them in your Life: for if you sow evil things, you shall reap all kind of trouble and affliction. Get Wisdom, in the fear of God, with diligence. For in case there happen a Captivity, and cities be destroyed, and countries, and gold, and silver, and all sorts of possession be destroyed, no one can take away the Wisdom of the wise Man: nothing can do that but the blindness of impiety, and the darkness of sin. Then will this Wisdom become to him matter of glory, among his enemies; and like his own country in a foreign land: and he will be discovered to be a friend in the midst of enemies. Whosoever shall teach these things and do them, he shall sit with a King; as did *Joseph* our brother.

§. 14. And now, My Sons, I know from the Scripture of *Enoch*, that in the end you will act impiously; laying hands upon the Lord in all wickedness: and your brethren will be ashamed of you; and you will be made a laughing stock to all the Gentiles. For your father *Israel* is pure from the impiety of the. High-Priests, who will lay their hands upon the *Saviour of the World*. The Heaven is purer than the Earth, and you are the luminaries of Heaven, as the Sun, and the Moon. What will all the Gentiles do, if you shall be darkened with impiety? and you will bring down a curse upon that flock of yours, upon which shall come that Light of the World, which shall be bestowed on you for the enlightening every Man. You will take it away, and you will teach commands opposite to the righteous Laws of God, you will steal the offerings of God, and take away by theft some of his portions; and you will take possession of the choice parts before you sacrifice to the Lord; and in contempt will eat [*them*] with harlots; and will teach the commands of the Lord out of covetousness: you will defile married women, and violate the chastity of the virgins of *Israel*; and will be joined with wicked and adulterous wives: you will [*also*] take the daughters of Gentiles for wives; purifying them with an illegal purification: and your accompanying with them will be as that of *Sodom* and *Gomorrha*, in impiety: and you will be puffed-up on account of your Priesthood, as elated in opposition to other Men. And not this only, but you will be puffed up in opposition to the commands of God: you Will make a jest of Holy things, laughing at them, with contempt.

§. **15.** For these causes, that very Temple which the Lord shall choose shall become desolate; and you shall be captives among all the

I Sam. ii. 12, &c.

Neh. xiii. 28, 29.

Psal. Solom. ii. 13, 14, 15. viii. 9—13. 24, 25.

57

Gentiles; and you shall be an abomination among them; and shall receive reproach and eternal shame from the righteous judgment of God; and all those that see you shall avoid you. And were it not for the sake of *Abraham*, and *Isaac*, and *Jacob* your fathers, not one,of your Seed should be left upon the Earth.

§. 16. And now I know what is in the Book of *Enoch*, that you will [*after that*] wander [*in error*} seventy weeks [*of years;*] and will profane the Priesthood, and pollute the Sacrifices, and will make the Law of none, effect, and will despise the words of the Prophets; in your perverse behaviour you will persecute righteous men, and hate the godly; you will abominate the words of those that speak truth; and you will declare that Man that comes to renew the Law, by the power of the Most High, to be an Impostor. And, at last, as you will suppose, you will slay him; without knowing of his resurrection: [*and*] you will receive innocent blood maliciously upon your Head. And for his sake, your Holy Place shall become desolate; being profaned to the foundation: and your place shall not be pure; but you shall be among the Gentiles for a curse, and for a dispersion; until the same person shall visit you again, and shall have compassion upon you, and shall receive you by faith and water.

§. 17. And since you have heard about the seventy weeks Hearken [*also*] about the Priesthood: for the Priesthood shall be according to every Jubilee. And in the first Jubilee, He that shall be first Anointed into the Priesthood shall be great, and shall speak to God as to a Father;

Dan. ix. 24, 25, 26.

Aaron.

and his Priesthood shall be complete, with the fear of the Lord: and in the day of his gladness he shall rise again for the Salvation of the World. He that shall be anointed in the second Jubilee shall be conceived in the sorrow of beloved [*Sons,*] and his Priesthood shall be honourable; and He shall be glorified by all. But the third Priest shall be assumed in sorrow. And the fourth shall be in troubles; for unrighteousness shall be laid upon him, and multiplied against him and all *Israel* shall hate every one his neighbour. The fifth shall be assumed in darkness; as also the sixth, and the seventh. But under the seventh shall be such a profanation as I am not able [*or permitted*] to express before the Lord, and before Men: for they that shall be the actors will know it. On account of which they shall be in Captivity, and be spoiled, and their land and their substance shall be brought to nothing. And in the fifth week [*of years*] they shall return to their Land, which was become desolate; and shall renew the House Of the Lord. But in the seventh septenary shall come Priests that shall be Idolaters, quarrelsome, lovers of money, proud, unjust, impure, *Sodom*ites and Buggerers.

§. 18. And after vengeance shall have been taken of these, by the Lord, and the Priesthood shall fail, the Lord will raise up a new Priest to whom all the words of the Lord shall be revealed. And He shall make a Judgment of Truth, in the fullness of days. And His Star shall arise, in Heaven, *as of a King*, affording light, the light of Knowledge, *above the Sun in the daytime.* And He shall be magnified in the whole World,

Samuel. 1 Sam. i.

Jehoiadab.

Jeremiah.

Joshua. Ezrah the Scribe. Jonathan. Vid. Joseph Antiq. XL. 7.

Under Ar- taxerxes Mnemon. 4 *Esd. x.* 45, 46.

Matt. ii. 2.

Ignat. ad Eph. §. 19.

until his assumption. *This person, shall shine as the Sun in the Earth. He shall take away all darkness, out of the lower World, and there shall be peace in all the Earth. The Heavens, shall leap for joy in his days; and the Earth shall be glad, and the Clouds shall rejoice, and the knowledge of the Lord, shall be poured out upon the Earth, as the water of the seas. And the Angels of Glory, and of the Presence of the Lord, shall rejoice in Him. The Heavens shall be opened; and out of the Temple of Glory, shall the Sanctification come upon Him, with the voice of his father, as [*it came*] * unto *Abraham*, the father of *Isaac*. And the glory of the Most High, shall be pronounced upon Him, and the Spirit of Understanding and of Sanctification, shall rest upon Him. By water shall He impart the glorious Gifts of the Lord to his Sons, in truth, for ever: and there shall be none to succeed to Him, from one generation to another, for ever. And under his Priesthood, the Gentiles shall be multiplied in knowledge, upon the Earth; and shall be illuminated, by the grace of the Lord. But *Israel*, shall be made little by their ignorance, and shall be darkened by their sorrow. And under his Priesthood, all sin shall fail, and the wicked shall leave off to afflict; but the righteous shall rest in him. For He shall open the gates of *Paradise* in and shall stop the threatening sword, that was placed against *Adam*; and shall give to his Holy Ones, to eat of the *Tree of Life*; and the *Spirit of Holiness* shall be upon them. And *Beliar* shall be *bound* by him; and He shall give power to his Children, to *tread upon all the wicked Spirits* and the Lord shall rejoice in his Children; and

The Messiah's first coming.
* *The Messiah's Second coming.*

* *Gr. from ἀπό for ἐπί.*
Matt. iii. 16, 17.
Gen. xxii. 11, 12. 15—18.

Gen. iii. 24.
4 Esd. viii. 52.
Gen. iii. 22.
Apoc. II. 7. XX. 1,2,3.
Luc. x.19.

the Lord shall be pleased with his beloved, for all ages. Then shall *Abraham*, *Isaac*, and *Jacob*, leap for joy: I also shall be glad, and all the Saints shall put on gladness.

§. 19. And now, My Sons, Ye have heard all. Choose therefore for your selves, either darkness or light; either the Law of the Lord, or the Works of *Beliar*. And we answered our father, saying, We will walk before the Lord, according to his law. And our father said, The Lord is witness; and his Angels are witnesses; and I am witness; and Ye are witnesses of this word of your mouth. And we said, They are witnesses. And thus *Levi* made an end of the Charge that he gave to his Sons: and he stretched out his feet and was gathered to his fathers: having lived 137 years. And they put him in a coffin, and afterward buried him in *Hebron*, near to *Abraham*, and *Isaac*, and *Jacob*. <abbr>*See Jos. XXIV.*</abbr>

J U D A S.

A copy of the words of *Judas*, which he spake to his Sons before he died. They gathered themselves together unto him; and he said unto them: I was my father's fourth Son; and my mother *Lea* named me *Judas*; saying, *I will give unto the Lord*, because he hath farther given me a fourth Son. I was quick and diligent in my youth, and obedient to my father in whatsoever he commanded me: and I honoured my mother, and my mother's father: and it came to pass as soon as I grew to man's estate, my father *Jacob* prayed for me, saying, Mayest thou be a King, prosperous in all things. *Gen. xxix. 35.*

§. 2. And the Lord gave me favour in all my works, both in the field, and at home. I perceived that I could keep pace with an hind: so I caught her, and made [*her*] meat for my father. I caught goats on the race; and I over-ran every creature that was in the plains. I overtook and caught a wild mare, and tamed her. I also slew a lion; and took a kid out of his mouth. I took a bear by the foot, and threw him down a precipice: and if any wild beast turned upon me, I tare it, as I would tare a dog. I kept pace with a wild boar and over-running him I tare him to pieces. A she-leopard had assaulted a dog in *Hebron*: I caught her by the tail, and threw her at a distance, and she was dashed to pieces, in the borders of *Gaza*. I caught a wild bull that was seeding in the country, by his horns; and swinging him about till I blinded him, then I threw him down, and slew him.

Vid. Gen. xlix. 8, 9.

§. 3. And when two Kings of the *Canaan*ites came upon the flocks armed, and much people with them, and I was alone, I ran upon the King of *Tyre*, and held him fast, and I tripped up his Legs, and threw him down, and so slew him. As for the other King of *Thaphue*, I slew him as he sat upon his horse; and by that means I dispersed all the people. I caught *Achor* the King, a Man that was a Giant, and shot his arrows both forward and backward; as he was on horseback; and I threw a stone of 60 pounds at his horse and slew him. And when I had fought with *Achor* for two hours I slew him and dividing his Shield into two parts, I cut off his Legs. Now as soon as I had plucked off his breastplate, behold eight Men, his companions, began to fight against me. So I wrapped up my garment in my hand, and flung stones at them; and slew four of them: upon which, the others ran away. Moreover, our father *Jacob* slew *Belisath*, the King of all Kings, a Giant in strength, of 12 cubits high. And trembling fell upon them, and they left off fighting against us. On this account my father was unconcerned in the battles, when I was with my brethren: for he saw in a Vision concerning me, that an Angel of power followed me in all occasions, that I might not be overcome.

§. 4. Moreover, we had a war on the South, greater than that at *Sychem*: wherein I encamped with my brethren, and pursued a thousand Men, and slew of them 200 Men, and four Kings. And I got up to them upon the wall, and slew two other Kings and so we set *Hebron* free; and we recovered all the Captives that those Kings had taken.

§. 5. And we went away the next day to another city, that was strong, and walled; and lay very near us, and threatened our death, I therefore, and *Gad*, made our approach on the far side of the city; while *Reuben* and *Levi* did it on the *West* and *South*. Now they that were on the wall, thinking that we were alone, gathered together from other places against us; so that my brethren came privately on each of their quarters, and ascended by the help of poles upon the walls, and entered into the city, while they were ignorant of it. And we took it by the edge of the sword: as also we took those that fled to the tower, upon Our burning that tower. And when we went away, the Men of *Thaphue* fell upon the Captives, whom we had taken: and they retook them with our children. Upon which we joined battle with them at *Taphue*, and slew them, and burnt the city, and took all that was in it as spoils.

§. 6. And when I was at the waters of *Chuzeba*, the inhabitants of *Jobel* came to us, to fight with us: and we joined battle, and slew them: we slew also those that came from *Selom*, their confederates, and gave them no opportunity to break in upon us. They also of *Mechir* came upon us on the fifth day, to retake our Captives: and we led our army against them, and beat them in an hard fight: for there were many strong Men among them: and we slew them before they could ascend up to that high ground where we were. But when we came to their city, their women rolled down stones upon us, from the top of the hill upon which the City stood. And I and *Symeon* hid our selves behind them, and took their heights, and destroyed the whole City.

§. 7. Moreover, on the next day we were informed, that the cities of two Kings were coming upon us, with a great company. Upon which, I and *Dan* pretending to be *Amorites* and auxiliaries, entered into their city; and in the dead of the night we opened the gates for our brethren, when they came and we took them all, and what they had for spoils; and overthrew their three walls. In *Thamna* also we made our approach, where all the treasure of the Kings that fought against us was reposited: at which time I received an affront, and was in a passion at it, and I rushed upon them with violence, at the top of the hill. They flung upon me with stones, and [*shot*] with bows: and had not my brother *Dan* came to my succour, they would have slain me. We came therefore upon them with fury, and they all fled. And passing by another way they came and begged of our father, and he made peace with them; and [*afterward*] we did them no harm: but made them our confederates, and restored all their Captives to them. Moreover, I built *Thamna* and my father [*built*] *Rambael*. I was 20 years old when this war happened: and the *Canaan*ites were afraid of me, and of my brethren.

§. 8. Now I had much cattle; and I had an head Shepherd, *Jeram* the *Odolamite*, to whom when I came, I saw there *Barsan* the King of *Odolam*. And he made us a feast; and at his desire I excepted of his Daughter *Bessue* to wife. And she bare me *Eir*, and *Aunan*, and *Silom*. Of which, God slew two, before they had any children: for *Silom* lived, and *you* are his children.

§. 9. Our father and we made a peace for 18 years with his brother *Esau*: and his Sons did the same with us, after we came out of *Mesopotamia*, from *Laban*: and at the end of those 18 years; in the 40th year of my life, *Esau*, my father's brother; came upon us, with an. heavy and strong force; and he fell by the bow of *Jacob* and was taken up [*for*] dead in mount *Seir*, and went up above *Eirramna* and died. And we pursued after the Sons of *Esau*. Now they had a City, and its walls were of iron, and its gates of brass; and we were not able to get into it: and we invested it round, and besieged it. And since they did not open their gates, after 20 days siege, I brought a ladder in their very sight, and [*held*] my shield over my

Pointing to that company of his sons that came of Silom.

Vid. Gen. xlviii. 22. and the small Genesis infrd.

Head; and I went up, and sustained stones as heavy as three talents: and when I was got up I slew four of their mighty Men: and the next day *Reuben* and *Gad* slew six more of them. Then they desired us to make peace with them: and having obtained the consent of our father, we received them as tributaries; and they always paid us 506 cores of Wheat: 500 baths of Oil: and 1500 measures of Wine; until we went down into *Egypt*.

§. 10. Now after this my Son *Eir* married *Thamar*, out of *Mesopotamia*, the Daughter of *Aram*. And *Eir* was wicked, and disputed with himself about *Thamar*; because she was not of the Land of *Canaan*: and the Angel of the Lord slew him, on the third day at night: and he knew her not, by the craftiness of his mother: for she would not that he should have children by her: and he died in his wickedness. And when it was proper to marry her again, I gave her to *Aunan*. He also in his wickedness did not know her: though he lived with her a year. And when I threatened him, he accompanied with her: but he spilled his Seed upon the ground; according to the injunction of his mother. I would also have given her *Silom* in marriage: but my wife *Bessue* would not permit me to do so: for she was ill-affected towards *Thamar*; because she was not of the daughters of *Canaan*, as she her self was.

§. 11. I knew indeed, that; the stock of *Canaan* was wicked: but the inclinations of youth blinded my mind. And when I saw her [*Bessue*] pouring out the wine, I was seduced by drinking too much wine; and I fell into her snares. This *Bessue*, in my absence, wept and took a wife for

Gen. xxii. 1.
Job. xxxii. 2.

Silom, but of the Land of *Canaan*. And when I knew what she had done, I cursed her, in the bitterness of my Soul; and she also died in the wickedness of her Sons.

§. **12.** Now after these things, while *Thamar* was a widow, she heard, after two years, that I Was going to shear Sheep; and adorning her self with wedding garments, she sat over-against the city, at the gate: for it was a Law of the *Amorites*, that a bride should sit publickly for fornication at the gate, for seven days. When, therefore, I was drunk at the water of *Chozeb*, I did not know who she was; on account of the wine I had drank. Her beauty also seduced me, by the form of her dress. And turning in unto her, I said, I will come in unto thee: and she said, What wilt thou give me? And I gave her my staff, and my girdle, and the diadem of my kingdom. And as soon as I had accompanied with her, she conceived. And not knowing what she had done, I would have had her slain. But when she had sent me the pledges privately, she put me to shame: and when I had called her, I made her repeat what I had said to her in secret, when I spake to her, as I lay with her in my drunkenness. And I was not able to slay her, for this thing was from the Lord. For I said, perhaps she does this in deceit, and has received the pledge from another woman. But I never approached to her again, unto my death. For what I had done was an abomination in all *Israel*. They also that were in the City said, there was not any harlot in that City; for she came from another place to sit for a while in the gate: supposing that no body knew that I had gone in

Gen. xxxviii. 13—26.

to her. Now after this, we came into *Egypt*, to *Joseph* on account of the famine. I was then 46 years old; and I lived there 73 years.

§. 13. And now what I say, I give you in charge: Hearken, My Sons, to your father *Judas*; and keep all these sayings, in order to your performing all the righteous laws of the Lord, to your obeying the. commands of God; and do not you follow your own desires, nor, the imaginations of your own thoughts, in the pride of your Heart; and do not you glory, in the actions of the virtue of your youth: for even this is evil in the eyes of the Lord. For I used myself to glory, that in the wars, the face of no beautiful Woman had seduced me; and I reproached *Reuben*, my brother, about *Bilha*, my father's wife. And the Spirit of Envy, and of Fornication, stood in array against me, until I fell upon *Bessue* the *Canaan*ite; and upon *Thamar* who had been married to my Sons. And I said to my father-in-law, I will consult my father, and so I will take thy daughter. And he shewed me an immense quantity of gold, to be given me With his daughter; for he was a King. He also, adorned her with gold and pearls, and ordered her to pour the wine out to us at the feast, [*so as best to shew*] the beauty of Women. And the wine perverted mine Eyes, and pleasure darkened my Heart; and falling in love with her, I yielded to her, and transgressed the command of the Lord, and the command of my fathers and took her to wife. And the Lord recompensed me according to the imagination of my Heart; for I had no joy in her sons.

§. 14. And now, My Sons, Be not drunk with wine; for wine perverts the Mind from the truth, and implants the passion of lust, and leads the Eyes into error. For the Spirit of Fornication uses wine as its instrument, for the pleasure of the Mind: for indeed both these take away the power of the Man: for if any one drink wine to drunkenness, he disorders his Mind, by filthy reasonings unto fornication; and inflames his Body for the obscene act and if an opportunity of lust present it self, he is guilty of the sin, and is not ashamed of it. This, My Sons, is the nature of wine, that the drunkard is ashamed of nothing; for lo, it seduced even Me, not to be ashamed of the multitude of the City; for I turned aside to *Thamar*, in the eyes of them all, and committed a great sin; and upon drinking the wine, I uncovered the covering, of the uncleanness of my Sons: I did not reverence the law of God, but took a *Canaan*ite Woman to wife. My Sons, He that drinks wine stands in needs of Understanding, and the Understanding that is necessary to the drinking of wine is this, that he drink no longer than his sense of shame remains; but if he goes beyond this bound, the Spirit of Deceit insinuates it self into his Mind, and makes the drunkard talk filthily, and break laws, and lay aside shame, nay, it makes him glory in his dishonour; supposing it to be a good thing.

§. 15. He that commits fornication, if he suffer loss, he feels it not; and is not ashamed when he loses his glory; For tho a Man were a King, and upon fornication were deprived of his Kingdom, he goes out as a slave to fornication; as I was [*thereby*] deprived [*of my honour;*] for I gave away my staff, that is the support of my tribe: and my girdle, that is my power: and the diadem, that is the glory of my kingdom. However, upon my repentance for these sins, I admitted into my mouth neither Wine nor flesh, unto my old age and I was a stranger to all pleasure. And the Angel of God shewed me, that so it would ever be; that when women prevail over any one, whether he be a King, or a poor Man, they will deprive the King of his glory the stout Man of his power;. and the poor Man of the last support of his poverty.

§. **16.** Observe therefore, My Sons, a measure in drinking wine: for in it there are four evil Spirits; the Spirit of Lust, of Inflammation, of Luxury, and of filthy Lucre. If you drink wine in gladness, and in the fear of God, and with a sense of shame, you shall live: but if you drink beyond the sense of shame, and without the fear of God; after that it is drunkenness: and together with that, impudence gets in. Nay, if you drink no Wine at all, you will avoid the sins of injury, and strife, and false accusation, and the transgression of the Law of God; and will prevent your perishing before your time. For truly, wine betrays the secrets of God and Men to foreigners: as I myself betrayed the commands of God, and the secrets of *Jacob* my father to *Bessue* the *Canaan*ite; to which [*Canaan*ites] God had said they should not be discovered. Wine is also the cause of war and of tumults.

§. **17.** I charge you, My Sons, not to love money; nor to look upon the beauty of Women: for even I myself went astray after *Bessue* the

*Canaan*ite, for money, and beauty. For I know that on account of these two my posterity will-be in wickedness: for they will pervert even the wise Men of my Sons, and will cause that kingdom of *Judah* to be diminished which the Lord gave me, for my obedience to my father: for I never in the least grieved my father *Jacob*: for I did whatsoever he bad me. And thus did my [*Great*] Grandfather *Abraham* bless me, that I should reign over *Israel. Isaac* also added his blessing to me, after the like manner. Wherefore I know, that the Kingdom shall be established out of me.

§. **18.** And I knew, by the Books of *Enoch* the Righteous, what wicked actions you will do in the last days. Keep your selves therefore, My Sons, from fornication, and from the love of money. Hearken to *Judas* your father: for these things separate Men from the Law of God, and blind the Counsels of the Soul, and teach pride, and suffer not a Man to have mercy on his neighbour: they deprive the Soul of all goodness and oppress him with troubles, and toils and take away his sleep; and feed upon his flesh; and hinder the Sacrifices of God and are unmindful of the benediction of God; and are disobedient to a Prophet, when he speaks and offend against the word of piety: for he that is a slave to two passions, which are contrary to the commands of God, cannot obey God: for they blind his Soul: and he walketh in the day time as in the night.

§. **19.** My Sons, The love of money leads the way to idols: for in deceit, on account of their silver, they name those Gods which are nothing. And it makes him that has the love of money to fail into a disorder of Mind, on account of that silver. I was the cause of the ruin of my Sons; and had it not been for the repentance of my flesh, and the humiliation of my Soul, and the prayers of *Jacob* my father, I had died childless. But the God of my fathers, who is compassionate and merciful, knew that I had committed [the sin] in ignorance. The prince of Error blinded me; and I was ignorant as a Man, and as flesh, when I was corrupted in sins: and I acknowledged my weakness, when I had supposed myself unconquerable.

§. 20. Know therefore, My Sons, that there are two Spirits attend upon a Man; The Spirit of Truth, and the Spirit of Error: and the Spirit of Understanding in the Mind is in the middle between them, to incline it self which way it will. Moreover, the principles of Truth, and those of Error, are written upon the breast of Man; and the Lord knoweth every one of them. Nor is there any time wherein the works of Man can be hidden [*from him*] for they are engraved in the breast of his hopes before the Lord. And the Spirit of Truth, bears witness of all things, and accuses of all things; and he that sins is burnt by the fire of his own Heart, and dares not lift up his face to his Judge.

§. 21. And now, My Sons, do you love *Levi*, that you may abide and do not elevate your selves against him; that you may not be destroyed. For the Lord hath given the Kingdom to me, and to him the Priesthood; and hath made the Kingdom subordinate to the Priesthood. To me hath he committed earthly affairs; and to him those that are heavenly. As the Heaven is superior to the Earth, so is the Priesthood of God superior to the earthly Kingdom; *[unless by sins he fall from the Lord, and be ruled over by that earthly Kingdom.]* For the Lord hath chosen him above thee to approach near to him, and to eat at his table, and of the first fruits of the delicious things of the children of *Israel*. *[But thou shalt be King of Jacob;]* and shalt be to them as the sea. For as therein the righteous and unrighteous are tossed in a tempest, while same are carried into slavery, and some will become rich; so will the state of mankind be with thee: some will be in danger in slavery; and others will grow rich by rapine. Those that reign will be like whales, who devouring Men as fishes, will enslave your freeborn Daughters and Sons; they will seize upon your houses, fields, and flocks, and money; and as ravens, and birds of prey, Will satiate themselves with the flesh of multitudes unjustly; and will proceed to wickedness, being exalted in their avarice. The false Prophets also will be like tempests, and will persecute all righteous Men.

§. 22. But the Lord will bring upon them, mutual quarrels, and perpetual wars shall be in *Israel* and my kingdom shall be put an end to, by aliens until salvation come to *Israel*, until the appearance of the God of Righteousness, to make *Jacob* to rest in peace, with all the Gentiles. And He shall keep the power of my kingdom for ever. For the Lord hath sworn with an oath unto me, that my kingdom shall not fail from my Seed, all the days, for ever.

§. 23. But I have great grief upon me, My Sons, on account of those instances of captivity uncleanness, and witchcraft, and idolatry, of which you will practice in that kingdom: following those that have familiar Spirits, and Divinations, and Daemons of Error. You will make your daughters singers, and you will expose them publickly; and you will intermix your selves with the abominations of the Gentiles; for which things, the Lord will bring upon you famine, and pestilence; death, and the sword; and a revenging siege; with dogs to tear you to pieces; reproaches both of enemies, and of friends destruction, putrefaction of your eyes; slaughter of infants; the loss of your wives; the ravage of your goods; the desolation of your land; the burning of the Temple of God; and your own slavery among the Gentiles. They will also castrate some of you, for Eunuchs to their wives; until you turn unto the Lord, with a perfect Heart; repenting, and walking in all the commandments of God. Then the Lord will visit you in Mercy; and will bring you back from captivity among the Gentiles.

§. 24. And after this, *A Star shall arise to you out of Jacob*, in peace; and a Man shall be raised up of thy Seed, as a *Sun of Righteousness*, conversing with the sons of Men, in meekness and Righteousness, and no sin shall be found in him. And the *Heavens shall be opened* upon him, to pour out the Spirit; the Blessing of his Holy Father. And He shall himself, pour out the Spirit of Grace upon you, and ye shall be to him sons in truth; and you shall Walk in his Precepts, both the first and the last. This is the *Branch* of the Most High God; and This is the *Fountain*, for the life of all flesh. Then shall the *Scepter* of my

of Babylon, for the two tribes.

2 King. xx. 18. Is. xxxix.7. Dan. i. 3, 7, 8, 9. The return from the Captivity of Babylon, of the two tribes. Num. xxiv. 17. Mal. iv. 2.

Matt. iii. 16. Act. ii.

Zech. Iii. 8. vi. 12.

kingdom shine forth, and a *Sprout* shall put forth from your root: and in him shall the rod of Righteousness ascend to the Gentiles, to judge and save all those that call upon the Lord.

§. **25.** And after this, *Abraham,* and *Isaac,* and *Jacob* shall rise again to life; with me, and my brethren, as Princes; and your scepter shall be over *Israel. Levi* shall be the first; I shall be the second; *Joseph* the third; the fourth *Benjamin:* the fifth *Symeon:* the sixth *Isachar:* and so all in their order. Now the Lord blessed *Levi:* an Angel of the Presence me: the Powers of glory *Symeon:* the Heaven *Reuben:* the Earth *Isachar:* the Sea *Zebulon:* the Mountains *Joseph:* the Tabernacle *Benjamin:* the Luminaries *Dan:* Delicacies *Nephthalim:* the Sun *Gad;* the Olive-tree *Aser:* and there shall be One people of the Lord, and One language: and there shall be no longer the Spirit of Deceit of *Beliar;* for he shall be cast into the Fire for ever. And those that died in sorrow, shall rise again in joy; and those that were in poverty for the Lord's sake shall be made rich: and those that were in want of food, shall have food enough; and those that were infirm, shall become strong: and those that died for the Lord's sake, shall be awakened out of their sleep in life; and the hinds of *Jacob* shall run with exultation, and the eagles of *Israel* shall fly about with joy. But the impious shall wail, and the sinners shall weep; and all the people shall glorify the Lord for ever.

§. **26.** Keep therefore, My Sons, all the Law of the Lord: for there is hope for all that walk strait along his paths. And he said unto, them, At 119 years of age I die this day, in your eyes. Let no

See, and hence correct our present Copies of Deut. xxxiii.

body bury me in precious clothing, or dissect my belly: for your King's will do such things: but bring me back to *Hebron* with you. And when *Judas* had said this, he fell asleep; and his Sons did to him according to all that he gave them in charge. And they buried him with his fathers, in *Hebron*.

I S A C H A R.

A copy of the words of *Isachar*. When he had called his Sons he said unto them: My Sons, Hear *Isachar* your father: Hearken to the words of him that was beloved of the Lord. I was born the fifth Son to *Jacob*, upon the hire of the *Mandrakes*. For *Reuben* brought *Mandrakes* [*Syrian Mauz*] out of the field, and *Rachel* meeting him took them. Now *Reuben* wept; and at his voice came out *Lea* his mother. These [*Mandrakes*] were Apples of a good smell, which the land of Syria produced on high, [*upon a very tall stalk,*] under the valley of waters. But *Rachel* said, I will not give thee these apples, for they shall be to me instead of Sons. Now there were two of them. And Lea said, Let it suffice thee that thou hast taken the husband of my virginity: wilt thou also take these [*apples*] also? But she said, Let *Jacob* be thine this night, instead of the Mandrakes of thy Son. But Lea said unto her, Do not boast, and do not vaunt thy self: *Jacob* is mine, and I am the wife of his youth. But *Rachel* said, How so: since he was first of all married to me; and on my account it was that he served our father fourteen years. What can be done in this case? since deceit and cunning prevails among

N.B. This must have been when they fed their flocks near Damascus. See the LXXII Josephus: & at large. Ludolphus Comment. In Hist. Aethiop. I. LXXII.

Men: [*and deceit prevails upon Earth*] otherwise thou hadst not seen the face of *Jacob*. For thou art not his wife, but by deceit wast introduced instead of me: and my father put a trick upon me; and removing me out of the way that night, suffered me not to see [*what was done;*] for had I been there, this matter had not been so carried. And *Rachel* said, Take one of the Mandrakes: and for the other, I do let him to hire to thee for one night. And *Jacob* knew *Lea*; and she conceived and bear me: and on account of this hire. I was called *Isachar*.

Gen. xxx. 18.

§. 2. Then did the Angel of the Lord appear to *Jacob*, saying, *Rachel* shall bear two Sons, because she refused the company of her husband, and chose chastity. And unless *Lea*, my mother, had parted with the two apples for his company, she had been permitted to bear eight Sons. But on that account she bear but six, and *Rachel* two: because the Lord visited her in the matter of the Mandrakes: for he saw that she desired the company of *Jacob* for the sake of Children, and not out of love to pleasure. For she let *Jacob* out to hire on the morrow, that she might have the other Mandrake. For this cause it was that the Lord heard *Rachel*, in the matter of the Mandrakes; because, though she desired them, she did not eat them, but dedicated them in the house of the Lord, and brought them to the Priest of the Most High, that was at that time.

§. 3. When therefore I grew up, My Sons, I walked in uprightness of heart; and I became the husbandman of my parents, and of my brethren; and I brought them the fruits of the ground in their seasons; and my father blessed me, seeing that I walked in an honest simplicity. I was not a busy-body in my actions, nor envious, nor malevolent to my neighbour. I spake evil of no body: nor did I carp at the life of any man: but walked in singleness of my eyes. For which cause I took me not a wife till I was thirty years of age; because my labour consumed my strength, and I did not think of pleasure with a woman: but sleep came upon me, by my taking such pains; and my father always rejoiced at my honest simplicity. And if I, by my labour, had gotten any fruit, and any thing first ripe, I offered it to the Lord, by the Priest; and then to my father; and then I partook of it myself. And the Lord doubled into my hands the good things I had done. Now *Jacob* knew that God was assisting to me in my honest simplicity: for I gave the good thing which the Earth produced to every one that was needy, and to every Man that was in distress, in singleness of heart.

§. 4. And now, Hear me, My Sons, and walk in an honest simplicity of heart; for I saw that therein was the entire method of pleasing God. He that is of a single heart desires not gold; does not exact of his neighbour; is not craving of variety of foods, does not covet variety of garments; does not promise to himself to live a long while; but does only expect the will of God. Even the Spirits of Error Will have ho power against him. For he hath no inclination to covet the beauty of a female, lest it should pollute his mind, to his overthrow. Spite will not come into his deliberations: envy does not make his Soul pine away, nor does he think of immoderate gain: but he Walks in uprightness of life: he sees all things sincerely, as they are, without the admission of wickedness at his eyes, from the deceit of the world that he may not have his sight perverted, as to any of the commandments of the Lord.

§. 5. Keep therefore, My Sons, the Law of God; and preserve this honest simplicity; and walk in innocence, Without being nicely inquisitive about the [reasons of the] commandments of the Lord, or about the actions of your neighbour. But love the Lord, and your neighbour, and be merciful to the needy, and the infirm. Submit your back to ploughing the Earth, and to painstaking in the labours of the ground; and at every season afforded by agriculture, offer your gifts to the Lord, with thanksgiving: for the Lord hath blessed thee in the first fruits of the Earth; *Gen. xlix. 14.* as he blessed all holy persons, from Abel to this time. For no other portion is allotted to thee, but the fatness of the Earth, from the husbandry of *Correct* which are its fruits derived: for our father *Jacob* *our copies* blessed me with the blessings of the Earth, and *of Genesis* of the first ripe fruits. And as for *Levi* and *Judah, hence.* they were glorified by the Lord, among the Sons of *Jacob.* For this they had moreover, that the Lord chose that his portion should be among them: and to one of them he gave the Priesthood, and to the other the Kingdom. Hearken to them, and walk in the honest simplicity of your father: [*and observe, that*] it is given to *Gad* to destroy the *v. 19.* temptations that shall come upon *Israel.*

§. 6. Now I know. My Sons, that in the last *Deut.* days our Sons will leave their honest simplicity, *xxxiii. 20,* and will adhere to insatiable covetousness: and *I Chr. xii.* forsaking their innocence, will approach to *8.*

wickedness; and laying aside the commandments of the Lord, Will adhere to *Beliar*; and leaving off husbandry, will follow evil Counsels of their own; and will be scattered abroad among the Gentiles, and will be in servitude among their enemies. Moreover, do you therefore tell these things to your Sons; that if they shall sin, they may quickly return to the Lord: for he is merciful, and will deliver them; that they may return to their own land.

§. 7. I am 122 years of age: and I never was conscious of any *sin unto death* in me. I never knew any woman, but my own wife: I was not guilty of fornication, in the elation of my eyes: I did not drink wine, to my deception: I did not covet any thing that was desirable, which was my neighbours: deceit was not in my heart: a lie never came within my lips: I consoled with every Man that was under grief; and I gave my bread to the poor. I did not eat alone: I did not remove a landmark: I Exercised myself to piety; and I acted with truth in all my days. I loved the Lord with all my might: in like manner I loved every man, as my children. Do you practice these things your selves also, My Sons; and every Spirit of *Beliar* will flee away from you; and no sort of practice of evil Men will have dominion over you. And you will bring every wild beast under; having with you the God of Heaven; conversing with Men in singleness of heart. And He charged them that they should carry him back to *Hebron* and there should bury him in the Cave of their fathers. And he stretched out his feet, and died, in a good old

I Joh. v. 16, 17.

age; having every member sound and strong: and he slept the eternal sleep.

Z A B U L O N.

A copy of what *Zabulon* delivered as his Testament, to his Sons, in the 114th year of his life, two years after the death of *Joseph*. And he said to them, Hear me, ye Sons of *Zabulon*, Attend to the words of your father. I am Zabulon, who was a good gift to my parents. For when I was born my father's estate was greatly increased, with flocks and herds when he had his wages by the various sorts of rods. I am not conscious, My Sons, that I have sinned in my days, any farther than thought: nor do I remember that I have perpetrated any wickedness, besides that sin of ignorance, which I was guilty of about *Joseph*: that i concealed what my brethren had done to him, so that I did not tell it to my father. But I wept bitterly in secret for *Joseph*. I was afraid of my brethren, because they had all agreed together, that if any one told the secret, he should be slain with the sword. However, when they were resolved to kill him, I greatly besought them, with tears, that they would nor perpetrate that wicked thing.

§. 2. For *Symeon* and *Gad* came upon *Joseph*, to kill him. And *Joseph* fell upon his face, and said to them, Have mercy on me, My Brethren: have compassion on the bowels of *Jacob* our father; do not lay your hands upon me, to shed innocent blood: for I have not sinned against you: But if I have sinned, correct and chasten me [*as brethren,*] but lay not your hands upon me, for

Gen. xxx. 20.

v. 28—43.

the sake of *Jacob* our father. Now as he said these words, I was moved with pity, and began to weep; and my bowels were greatly moved within me; and all my inward parts were loosed upon my Soul. Now *Joseph* wept, and I wept with him; my Heart made a noise, and the joints oi my Body were loosed, and I was not able to stand. And when he saw that I wept with him, and that they were coming upon him to kill him, he ran behind me; begging of them [*to spare him.*} Then *Reuben* said, Brethren, Let us not kill him; but let us cast him into one of these dry pits, which our fathers dug, and found no water. For on this account the Lord had forbidden water to rise up in it, that it might afford a refuge to *Joseph*. And the Lord did so, until they sold him to the *Ishmaelites*.

§. 3. For I did not myself partake of the price of *Joseph*, My Sons; but *Symeon*, and *Gad*, and six other of my brethren. And they took the money for which *Joseph* was sold, and bought shoes for themselves, and for their wives, and their children saying, It is the *price* of the *blood* of our brother; and we will not eat it, but treading we will tread it under our feet: on account of what he said, that he should reign over us and we shall see what his dreams will come to. For which cause it is written in the Scripture of the Law of *Enoch*, that He who will not *raise up Seed to his brother*, his shoe shall be loosed, and they shall spit in his face. Now the brethren of *Joseph* would not save the life of their brother, and the Lord loosed their shoe, which they had worn against *Joseph* their brother. For when they came into *Egypt* their *shoes were loosed* by the servants

Matt. xxvii. Constitut. IV. 10.

See Deut. xxv. 7, &c.

of *Joseph*, before the gate: and so they worshipped *Joseph*, as they used to worship *Pharaoh*. Nay, they did not only worship him, but they were also *spit* upon, when they fell down before the *Egyptians*. For after this the *Egyptians* heard, of all the evils which we had done to *Joseph*.

§. 4. When they had done this, they set down to eat: for I had not eaten of two days and nights; as moved with bowels of compassion for *Joseph*. *Judas* also did not eat with them: for his attention was upon the pit: for he was afraid lest *Symeon* and *Gad* should return back and kill him. And when they saw that I did not eat neither, they set me to keep him, till he were sold. Now he continued in the pit three days and three nights, and was sold fasting. And *Reuben*, when he heard that he was sold in his absence, he rent his cloths, and lamented, saying, How shall I see the face of *Jacob* my father? And taking money, he ran after; the Merchants; but did not find them: [*for*] they had left the great road, and were gone by the *Troglocolpita*, which Was a nearer way. And *Reuben* eat no bread that day. Whereupon *Dan* came to him, and said, Do not weep or lament; for I have thought of a thing that we, may say to our father *Jacob*. We will slay a kid of the goats, and we will dip *Joseph*'s coat in it, and will say, Consider whether this be thy Son's coat or not: for they had plucked our father's coat off *Joseph*, when they were going to sell him, and had put on him an old servant's garment. But *Symeon* had the coat, and would not give it them: as resolving to cut it to pieces, in his rage, because he was still alive; and because he had

Test. Jos. §. I.

Test. Benj. §. 2.

83

not killed him. But we all rose up together, and said, If thou wilt not give it us we will say. It was thou alone that didst this wicked, thing, before the Lord, in *Israel*. Upon which he gave it: and they did as *Dan* had said.

§. 5. And now, My Sons, I give you warning, that you keep the commandments of the Lord, and execute mercy towards your neighbour, and have compassion towards all creatures, not only towards men, but also towards to the brute beasts. For it Was on this account that the Lord blessed me: and when all my brethren were sick, I escaped without sickness: for the Lord knew every one of our purposes. Have therefore mercy in your bowels, My Sons, for according to what any one does to his neighbour, so will the Lord do to him. For the Sons of my brethren were sick and died, on account of *Joseph*, because they did not retain mercy in their bowels [*for him;*] but my Sons were preserved without sickness, as you know. And when we were in the land of *Canaan*, by the sea shore, I went a fishing for draughts of fish, for my father *Jacob*: and when many were choked in the sea, I continued unhurt.

Prov. xii. 10.

§. 6. I was the first who made a boat, to sail in the sea: for the Lord gave me Understanding and Wisdom in that matter; and I let down a piece of wood behind it, [*for the rudder:*] and I spread out a piece of cloth upon a strait piece of wood in the middle, [*for a sail:*] and going along the shores I fished for the house of my father, until we came into *Egypt*: and out of what I caught I gave out of pity to every one that was a stranger. But if any such Stranger were sick, or in years, I boiled the fishes, and prepared them as well as I could, and carried them to all, according as every one had need: taking them in, and condoling with them. And for this reason it was, that the Lord made me catch great draughts of fishes. For he who gives to his neighbour, receives it manifold from the Lord. I fished five years; giving thus to every man whom I saw; and supplying the whole house of my father therewith. I fished in summer; and in winter I fed the flocks, with my brethren.

§. 7. I will now inform you what I did. I saw a man in distress with nakedness in winter; and taking pity of him, I privily; stole a garment out of my own house, and gave it to the man in distress. And therefore do you, My Sons, take pity of all that are in distress, without distinction: and out of what God bestows upon you, bestow it upon every man with a good heart. And it, for some time, you have not any thing to give to any one that is in want, have compassion on him in the bowels of mercy. I am conscious, that once my hand did not find any thing to give to one that was in Want; yet still I went along with him seven furlongs, and wept, and my bowels were moved to companion for him.

§. 8. And therefore have you, My Sons, compassion towards every Man, with mercy; that the Lord may have compassion towards you; and have mercy upon you. For even God will, in the last days, send his bowels of compassion upon the Earth: and where he shall find bowels of mercy, in him will he dwell: for to what degree a Man Exerciseth compassion towards his neighbour, to the same degree will the Lord Exercise compassion towards him. For when we came down into *Egypt, Joseph* did not remember the injuries we had done him, to our disadvantage: but when he saw me he shewed his compassion towards me. And in consideration of his example, do not you keep injuries in mind, My Sons, and do you love one another, and let not any one of you impute evil to his brother: for that divides unity, and disorders all ties of consanguinity, and disturbs the Soul: for he that is mindful of injuries has not bowels of mercy.

§. 9. Take notice of waters, that when they go the same way, they carry along with them stones, and wood, and sand: but if they are divided into several currents, the Earth drinks them up, and they become contemptible. So also will it be with you, if you fall into divisions. Do not you separate your selves into two Heads: for whatsoever the Lord hath made, hath but one Head. He hath given us two shoulders, feet, and hands; but all the members are subject to one Head. I know by the Scripture of our fathers, that in the last days, you will apostatize from the Lord, and will be, divided in *Israel*, and will follow two Kings, and will do every thing that is, abominable: nay, you will worship every idol also: and your enemies will carry you into captivity; and you will sit down among the Gentiles, under all sorts of infirmities, and afflictions, and griefs of Soul., And after this, you will be mindful of the Lord, and you will repent and he will cause you to return: for He is merciful, and compassionate; not imputing evil to the Sons of Men, because they are flesh, and the Spirits of Error deceive them in all their afflictions, And after these things, the Lord himself will raise up the *Light of righteousness*, and there will be *healing* and commiseration *on bis wings*. He will himself redeem all the captivity of the Sons of Men, from *Beliar*; and every Spirit of Error shall be trodden down; and he shall convert all the Gentiles to have a zeal for him; and ye shall see a God in the form of a Man, in *Jerusalem*, which the Lord will so name. And again, you will provoke him to anger with the wickedness of your Words; [*actions*;j and ye shall be cast away, till the time of consummation.

Mal. iv. 2.

§. **10.** And now, My Sons, Be not grieved that I die: neither be ye cast down, because I leave you. For I shall arise again in the midst of you, a Ruler in the midst of my Sons; and I shall rejoice in the midst of my tribe, as many as have kept the law of the Lord, and the commands of Zabulon their father. But upon the ungodly the Lord will bring eternal fire, and will destroy them for [*several*] generations; I go away to my rest, as my fathers did. But do you fear the Lord your God, with all your might, all the days of your life. And when he had said this, he slept a good sleep; and his Sons put him in a coffin; but afterward they brought him back to *Hebron*, and buried him with his fathers.

D A N.

A copy of the words of which he spake to his Sons in his last days, in the 125th year of his life. And when he had called his family about him, he said; Hear my words, Ye Sons of *Dan*; attend to the words of the mouth of your father; I tried in my heart, and in all my life, what was good and pleasing to God; Truth and Righteous Practice; and that Lying and Anger, are evil, and teach Men all sorts of wickedness. I confess to you this day, My Sons, that I was glad at heart when the death of *Joseph* [*was designed:*] who was a Man of goodness, and truth. And I rejoiced at the selling of *Joseph*, because our father loved him above us: for the Spirit of Envy and Pride, said to me, Thou art also his son; and one of the Spirits of *Beliar* co-operated with me, saying, Take this sword, and therewith slay *Joseph*; and when he is dead thy father will love thee. This is the Spirit of Anger, which persuaded me, that as a leopard sucks the blood of a kid, so should I suck that of *Joseph*. But the God of my father "*Jacob* did not let him fall into my hands; nor did I meet with him when he was alone: nor did he permit me to dissolve two of the tribes of *Israel*.

§. **2.** And now, My Sons, I die; and I tell you in truth, that unless you keep your selves from the Spirit of Lying, and of Anger, and love truth, and meekness, you shall perish. There is a blindness in anger, My Sons; and there is no passionate Man that can see another's face as it truly is. For if he be a father, or a mother, he considers them as enemies: if he be a brother, he does not know him: if he be a *Prophet* of the Lord he regards him not: if he be a *Righteous Man*, he does not look upon him: nor does he acknowledge his friend: for the Spirit of Anger spreads the nets of error about him, and blinds his natural eyes. By lying he darkens his

2 Bar. Postsc. I.4. Herm. Simil. IX. §. 15. Matt. x. 41. Xiii. 17.

Understanding, and gives him his own sight. But wherein does he blind his eyes? By hatred of heart. Moreover, he gives him his own heart, full of envy against his brother.

§. 3. Anger is wicked, My Sons: for it becomes a Soul to the Soul itself, and makes the body the same with that of the passionate [*Spirit.*} It also domineers over the Soul, and gives a peculiar force to the body, that it may perpetrate all sorts of iniquity: and when the Soul has acted, it justifies what has been done; because it sees not. Wherefore, he that is angry, if he be strong, has three times the strength in his anger: one part by reason of the strength and assistance of those that minister to him; a second part by reason of his riches, persuading and overcoming by unjust methods; a third part is the natural strength of his body; while of himself he does the evil action. But although the angry Man be weak in body, yet hath he a double strength, Besides that from nature: for anger always assists the other in transgression. This Spirit does always go with falsehood at the right hand of Satan; that his actions may be done with cruelty and lying.

§. 4. Wherefore do ye understand the strength of anger, that it is vain. For at first it provokes by words, and then fortifies him that is angry by deeds; and by bitter losses disturbs his deliberations; and by such means it put his Soul into a great passion. When therefore any one speaks against you, be not you moved to anger: and if any one commend you, as good Men, be not elevated thereat: nor do you change your temper either to overmuch delight [*in the one,*] or uneasiness [*at the other.*] For the first [*only*] pleases the hearing: and [*the second*] excites the mind to attend to the quarrel, and then falling into a rage, the Man thinks he has reason to be angry. And although any loss or misfortune should befall you, My Sons, be not disturbed: for the same Spirit makes you desirous of what you have lost, that you may by that desire be put into a passion. But if you suffer any loss voluntarily, be not troubled: for from that trouble passion is stirred up, with lying. This evil has two faces, Passion with Lying, which conspire together, to disorder the mind. Now when the Soul is continually disordered, the Lord departs from it; and *Beliar* has dominion over it.

§. 5. Keep therefore the commandment of the Lord, and observe his Law: but depart from anger, and hate lying; that the Lord may inhabit in you; *Speak every one truth to his neighbour*, and ye shall not fall into wrath and disturbances, but you shall be in peace; and have the God of peace; and war shall not prevail against you. Love the Lord in all your life; and one another, with a true heart. For I know that in the last days, you will depart from the Lord, and will be enemies to *Levi*, and will oppose *Judas*: but you will not be able to prevail against them. For the Angel of the Lord guides each of them, because by them, *Israel* shall be established. And as soon as ye depart from the Lord, you will walk in all wickedness, and do the abominations of the Heathen; committing fornication with the wives of the wicked: while the Spirits of Error operate in you, in all kind of wicked practice. For I have read in the book of *Enoch* the Righteous, that your Ruler is Satan; and that all the Spirits, both

Eph. iv. 25, 26.

those of Fornication, and those of Pride, will obey *Levi*, [*a false copy*,] in order to lay snares for the Sons of *Levi*, to make them sin before the Lord. And my Sons will come near to *Levi*, and will sin with them in all things: and the Sons of *Judas* will be in covetousness, seizing upon others goods, like lions. For which cause you shall be led with them into captivity, and there shall you receive all the plagues of *Egypt*, and all the wickedness of the Gentiles. And when you shall return to the Lord, you shall have mercy vouchsafed to you: and He shall lead you to his Sanctuary, and proclaim peace to you. *And the Salvation of the Lord shall arise to you out of the tribe of Judah and Levi:* and he shall make war against *Beliar*, and he shall afford the vengeance of his victory to your borders. And he shall take away from *Beliar*, the Souls of the Saints, as captives, and still *convert the disobedient hearts to the Lord;* and still bestow eternal peace on those that call upon him. And the Saints shall rest in Eden: and the Righteous shall rejoice in the New *Jerusalem*: which shall be for the glory of God, for ever. And *Jerusalem* shall no more undergo desolation: nor shall *Israel* be carried captive: for the Lord shall be in the midst of her, converting with men; and the Holy one of *Israel* shall reign over them, in humility and poverty. And he that believeth in him shall reign in truth, in the Heavens.

§. **6.** And now fear ye the Lord, My Sons; and take care of your selves, to avoid Satan, and his Spirits. But draw near to God, and to the Angel that pleads for you; for He is the Mediator of God and Men, for the peace of *Israel*. He will stand against the Kingdom of the Enemy. For

Ex. xv. 26, 27.
Deut. xxvii. 27, 59, 60, 61. vii. 15.

Gen. xlix. 18.

Histor. Abgar. Luk. 1. 17.

Apoc. XXI. 2.

Test. Levi, §. 5.

which reason the Enemy earnestly endeavours to subvert the steps of all that call upon the Lord. For he knoweth, that in the day that *Israel* shall believe, the Kingdom of the Enemy shall be ended. He is the Angel of peace, and will strengthen *Israel*, that he may not fall into the extremity of evils. Now the Lord will depart from them in the day of the iniquity of *Israel* but will return again to him that doth his will: [*for none of the Angels shall be like him:*] His name in every place of *Israel*, and among the Gentiles shall be the SAVIOUR Keep your selves therefore, My Sons, from every wicked work; and cast away from you anger, and all lying; and love truth, and long suffering: and what you have heard of your father do you also deliver down to your Sons; that the Father of nations may receive you. For he will be true, and long suffering, meek, and humble; teaching by his actions the Law of God. Depart therefore from all unrighteousness; and adhere to the Righteousness of the Law of God; and my flock shall be for Salvation for ever. And bury me near my fathers.

Math. i. 21.

§. 7. And when he had said this, he kissed them; and slept the eternal sleep. And his Sons buried him; and afterward they brought back his bones, [*and laid them*] near to *Abraham, Isaac, and Jacob.* But as *Dan* prophesied to them, that they would forget the Law of their God, and should be driven out of the land of their inheritance, and of the flock of *Israel*, and of their own country, so it came to pass. [*An Addition afterwards.*]

NEPHTHALIM.

A copy of the Testament of Nephthalim, which
he made at the time of his end, in the 130th [or
132nd] year of his life. When his Sons came together, in the eleventh month, on the fourth day of
the month, *as he was in health*, he made them a
supper, and a feast: and after he awaked in the
morning he said to them, I am about to die: and
they did not believe him: and he blessed the
Lord, and confirmed it, that after supper the next
day he should die. Accordingly, he began to say
to his Sons, Hear, My Sons, Ye Sons of
Nephthalim, Hear the words of your father. I
was born of *Bilha*h: and because *Rachel acted
cunningly*, and gave *Bilha*h to *Jacob* instead of her
self, and she bare me upon the thighs of *Rachel*,
on that account was I called Nephthalim. And
Rachel loved me, because I was born upon her
thighs, and she kissed me, who was a child of a
delicate aspect, and she said, May I see a brother
of thine, of my own womb, after thee. Whence it
was that *Joseph* was like to me in all things,
according to the prayers of *Rachel*. But my
mother is *Bilha*h the daughter of *Ruthaeus*, the
brother of *Deborah*, *Rebecca*'s *nurse*: and she was
born the same day that *Rachel* was born. Now
Ruthaeus was of the stock of *Abraham*, a *Chaldean*,
one that feared God, free, and well born. And he
having been carried captive, was redeemed by
Laban: and he gave him *Enan* his maid servant to
wife: who bear him a daughter, and called her
Zelpha, from the name of the village out of
which she was carried captive. And after this she
bare *Bilha*h; saying, Thou art very quick, my

*See Deut.
xxxiv. 7.*

*Gen. xxx.
8.
See also
Josephus.*

*Gen.
xxxvi. 8.*

daughter: for as soon as ever she was born, she hastily sucked.

§. 2. And because I was light of feet, as an hind, my father *Jacob* appointed my employment, to go on every errand and message: and accordingly He blessed me, as *an hind*. For as a Potter knows his vessel, how much it is to hold; and in proportion to it brings the clay; so does the Lord make the Body, according to the likeness of the Spirit; and inserts the Spirit, according to the power of the Body; and there is no defect as to the one or the other; to the third part of an hair. Every creature of the Most High, is according to *weight and measure, and rule*: and as the potter knows the use of every one of his vessels, of what capacity [*or strength*] it is, so does the Lord know the Body, how far it will reach, in doing right; and where it begins to do wrong. For there is nothing created no cogitation which the Lord does not know: for he *made every Man according to his own image*. As is his ability, so is his work; and as is his mind, so also is his work; and as is his purpose, so is his practice; as is his heart, so is his mouth; as is his eye, so is his sleep as is his soul, so is his word, either in the law of the Lord or in the law of *Beliar*: and as there is a difference between light and darkness; between sight and hearing; so is there a difference between Man and Man, between Woman and Woman: and one cannot say that in any one thing, or in any one feature of their face, they are exactly alike. For God made all things in order, [*and made them*] good. He put the five senses in the head; he connected the neck to the head and gave him hair for beauty and glory;

Gen. xlix. 21.

Wisd. xi. 20.

Gen. i. 26, 27.

94

and Besides, he gave him an heart for understanding; a belly for separation of the stomach; the *reed* for health; the liver for passion; the bile for bitterness the spleen for laughter; the reins for cunning; the muscles of the loins for strength; the ribs for the chest; the spine for power; and so of the rest. After the like manner, My Sons, Be ye in a good order, in the fear of God; and do ye nothing that is disorderly, and from contempt nor out of its proper time. If thou shouldest say to thine eye, Hear; It cannot do it: nor can it in darkness do the works of light.

§. 3. Do not you therefore endeavour by covetousness to destroy your actions, or to deceive your own Souls, by vain words: for by silently going on in purity of heart, you will be able to observe the will of God, and to reject the will of the Devil. The Sun, and the Moon, and the Stars do not change their order. Accordingly, neither do you change the Law of God, by the disorder of your practices. The Gentiles have gone astray; and, leaving the Lord, have changed their order, and have followed after stones and wood, by following the Spirits of Deceit. But do not you do so, My Sons: as knowing that in the firmament, in the earth, in the sea, and in all parts of the creation there is the Lord that made all things: that you may not become like *Sodom*, which changed the order her nature. *In like manner* did the *Egregori* change the order of their nature; whom the Lord cursed at the flood; appointing that, for their sakes, the Earth should be desolate, without inhabitants, and fruits.

Some mistake in the Copies.

Jude, v. 6, 7.

95

§. 4. I say this, My Sons, because I know, by the Holy Scripture of *Enoch* that ye will your selves also depart from the Lord; walking according to all the wickedness of the Gentiles: and will do according to all the iniquity of *Sodom*: and the Lord will bring upon you captivity and you will serve your enemies and you will be overwhelmed with all sorts of adversity and affliction; until the Lord destroy you all. And after you are diminished, and become few in number, You will return, and will acknowledge the Lord your God, and he will bring you back unto your Land, according to his great mercy. And it will come to pass, that when they shall come unto the Land of their fathers, they will again forget the Lord, and Will act wickedly; and the Lord will scatter them upon the face of the whole Earth; until the compassion of the Lord come; a Man that doth Righteousness, and exerciseth mercy towards all Men, both *those that are far off and those that are nigh.*

By Ben-hadad. 1 *King.* *xv.* 20. 2 *Chr. xvi.* 4.

By Tal-gath-Pul-Assar. 2 *King.* *xv.* 29. 1 *Chr. v.* 26. *Eph. ii.* 17.

§. 5. For in the 40th year of my life, I saw, in a dream, in the mountains of *Olives*, on the *East of Jerusalem*, that the Sun and the Moon stood still: and behold *Isaac* my father's father said to us Run every one of you, and catch them; according to your abilities: and the Sun and Moon shall belong to him that can catch them. And we all ran together: and *Levi* caught the Sun; and *Judas* made haste and caught the Moon: and they were both exalted with them. And as *Levi* appeared like the Sun, a certain young Man gave him the branches of 12 Palm-trees, *Judas* also was splendid, like the Moon; and under his feet, were 12 Rays. And *Levi* and *Judas* ran into one another's arms, and caught one another. And behold there was a Bull upon the Earth, having two great horns, and the wings of an Eagle upon his back: and when we would have caught him, we could not. But *Joseph* made haste and caught him and went up with him on high. And I saw (for I was there present myself) and behold an *Holy Scripture* appeared to us, that said, The *Assyrians*, the *Medes*, the *Persians*, the *Elamites*, the **Chelcites*, the *Chaldeans*, and the *Syrians*, shall possess in Captivity the twelve tribes of *Israel*.

*The People of Chalach.
2 King. xvii. 6. xviii. II. 1 Chr. v. 26.

§. 6. Again, seven months afterwards, I saw our father *Jacob* standing at the sea of Jamnia, and we his Sons were with him: and lo a ship came under sail, full of salt flesh; without either mariners, or a steers-man: the ship had this inscription, *Jacob's Ship*. And our father said to us, Let us go up into our ship: but as soon as we were got into it, there happened a great storm, and a mighty whirlwind; and our father who held the helm flew away from us; and we were carried away with the tempest into the sea, and the ship was filled with waters, and was dashed with vast waves, till it was broken to pieces. And *Joseph* fled away in the boat: and we were all accordingly separated, upon ten planks but *Levi* and *Judas* were upon the same plank. We were therefore scattered about, in the last extremity. But *Levi* put on sackcloth, and prayed for us all to the Lord. Now as soon as the storm ceased, the boat came to land, as in a calm: and our father *Jacob* came to us, and we unanimously rejoiced together.

§. 7. I told these two dreams to my father: and he said to me, They must be fulfilled in their seasons, in the great sufferings of *Israel*. Then said my father, I believe that *Joseph* is alive: for I see always that the Lord numbers him together with you: and he said with tears, Dost thou live, My son *Joseph*, and dost thou not see thy father *Jacob*? and he made us all weep with his words. And I burned in my bowels to tell him that he was sold but I was afraid of my brethren.

§. 8. Behold, My Sons, I have shewed you the last times, when all shall be accomplished in *Israel*. Do you therefore also charge your Sons, that they be united to *Levi*, and to *Judas*: for through *Judas* shall salvation arise unto *Israel*: and in him shall *Jacob* be blessed: for by his tribe, shall God appear, inhabiting among Men upon Earth, to save the flock of *Israel*: and he will gather the righteous of the Gentiles together. For *Gen. xlix. 10.* if you do good works, My Sons, both Men and Angels will Bless you; and God will he glorified among the Gentiles through you; and the Devil will flee away from you; and the wild Beasts will be afraid of you; and the Angels will adhere to you. As when any one educates his Son well, he has a good memorial; so it is with a good work, its good memorial is with God. But as to one that does no good work, both Angels and Men will curse him; and God will be dishonoured among the Gentiles through him.; and the Devil will possess him as his own vessel; and every wild beast will have dominion over him; and the Lord will hate him. For the commandments of the law are double: there is a time of accompanying with a man's wife; and a time of abstinence, for his prayer; these two commands are such, that if they be not done in their order they procure sin: and so it is in the rest of the commandments. Be ye therefore wise in God, and prudent; knowing the order of his commands, and the measures of. every action, that the Lord may love you.

§. **9.** And when he had given many such things in charge to them, he exhorted them that they should carry his bones unto *Hebron*, and bury him with his fathers. And when he had eaten, and drunk, in the gladness of his Soul, he covered his face and died: and his Sons did according to all things, which *Nepthalim* their father charged them to do.

Eccles. lii. 5.
1 Cor. vii. 5.

G A D.

A copy of the Testament of *Gad*, what he spake to his Sons in the 125th year of his life. I was the seventh Son of *Jacob*; I was a stout Man in keeping the flocks. I kept the flock in the night-time; and when a wolf, or a lion, or a leopard, or a bear came upon the flock, I followed him; and catching him by the foot with my hand, and whirling him about, I blinded him; and throwing him as *far as two furlongs, I, by that that means, slew him. Now *Joseph* fed the flock with us about 30 days; and being one of a tender constitution, was disordered by the heat, and returned to *Hebron* to his father: and he made him lie near to himself: for he loved him. And *Joseph* said to our father, that the Sons of *Zilpha*, and *Bilha*h, sacrificed good creatures, and eat

* At Seve-ral times.

them also, contrary to the direction of *Judas* and *Reuben*. For he saw that, I took a lamb out of the mouth of a bear, and killed the bear, and sacrificed the lamb: (for which I greatly grieved that it could not live:) and we eat it; and he told our father of it: and they had indignation against *Joseph* for this thing, until the Very day that he was sold into *Egypt*. And the Spirit of Hatred was in me; and I would not see *Joseph* with my eyes, Or [*hear him*] With my ears. He also reproved us to our face, that we eat the young ones of the flock without *Judas*: and whatsoever he said to his father, he was persuaded of him.

§. **2.** I confess now my sin, My Sons, that I would many times have slain him For I hated him at my very Soul: and I had no manner of bowels of compassion for him. And, indeed, I hated him still more for his dreams, and would have licked him up out of the land of the living, as a calf licks up the green herbs from the Earth. Wherefore I and *Judas* sold him to the *Ishmaelites* for 30 pieces of gold of which we concealed 10, and shewed the other 20 to our brethren. And so covetousness made me exceeding ready to have him taken out of the way. But the God of my fathers delivered him out of my hand; that I might not perpetrate wickedness.

§. **3.** And now, Hear the words of truth, that you may do Righteousness, and [*keep*] every Law of the Most High. And do not ye wander about with the Spirit of Hatred: for it is an evil thing in all the actions of Men. Whatever a malicious Man does he is abominable. If he do the Law of the Lord, God does not praise him: if he fears the Lord, and would do what is right,

Gen. xxxvii. 5—11.

v. 28. See Vulg. & Sept. & Jos.

God does not love him. He carps at truth; he envies a Man that prospers; he embraces evil-speaking; and he loves pride. For malice hath blinded his Soul: as I saw in the case of *Joseph*.

§. 4. Keep your selves therefore, My Sons, from hatred: for it works iniquity against the Lord himself: for it will not hear the words of his commands, concerning the love of our neighbour, and it sins against God: for if his brother offend, he desires presently to tell it to all, and hastens the judgment concerning him, and his punishment unto death. But if the offender be a servant, he accuses him to his Lord: and in all his affliction he rejoices against him, if by any means he may bring him to death. For hatred cooperates to murder: and when any do well, and are in prosperity, and he either hears it or sees it, he is sick upon it. For as love would revive even those that are dead, and recall them back that are under the sentence of death; so would hatred slay those that are alive, and would not have those that have been guilty of venial sins to live any longer. For the Spirit of Hatred is so narrow of Soul, that it co-operates with Satan in all things, for the death of Men: but the Spirit of Love, by long-suffering co-operates with the Law of God, unto the Salvation of Men.

§. 5. Hatred is therefore an evil thing, because it always abides with lying; speaking against truth; and makes small offenses great: it darkens light: it calls sweet bitter: and teaches calumny, and war, and, injury, and all sorts of evil desires: and fills the heart with diabolical poison. I speak this by experience, that you may avoid hatred, and may adhere to the love of the Lord.

Righteousness casts out hatred; humility takes away hatred: for the righteous and the humble Man is ashamed to do an unjust thing not as reproved by another, but by his own heart; for the Lord preserves his Will. He does not speak against any [*holy*] Man, because the fear of God overcomes his hatred: for being afraid of offending the Lord, he will not, in the least, injure any Man; no, not in his thoughts. This I knew at last, after my repentance concerning *Joseph*: for that true *repentance*, which *is according to God*, takes away disobedience, and drives away darkness, and enlightens the eyes, and affords knowledge to the Soul, and guides the will to salvation. It does not learn from Men; but knows it by repentance: [*that those those that are converted will be received.*] For God brought upon me a distemper in my bowels and had it not been for the prayers of my father *Jacob*, my Spirit had failed, and I had died. For by those things wherein a Man transgresses is he also punished. Therefore because my bowels were unmercifully disposed against *Joseph*, I was condemned to suffer unmercifully in my bowels, for eleven Months: which was the same length of time that I watched for the sale of *Joseph*.

§. 6. And now, My Sons, Do you every one love his brother; and take away hatred from your hearts: loving one another in deed, and in word, and in the affection of your heart; for before our father's face, I spake kindly to *Joseph*: but when I was gone out of his sight, the Spirit of Hatred blinded my mind, and disordered my Soul; so that I endeavoured to slay him. Do you

2 Cor. vii. 9. 10. 11.

therefore love one another from your heart: and if any one sin against thee, speak to him peaceably; banishing all the poison of hatred; and do not retain deceit in thy Soul: and if he *confess his fault, forgive him*: and though he deny it, do not contend with hm, lest he swear, and thou be guilty of a double sin. Let not a stranger in your contests, hear any of your secrets; that he may not hate and malign thee, and work a great sin against thee: for he will slay thee secretly, and will privately enquire out your affairs, for mischief: as having got poison from thee. But if he deny his offense, and is ashamed when he is reproved, and keep silence, do not thou expose him. For he that denies his offense, is sorry for it: so that he will not repeat it towards thee; but will have a respect for thee, and will be afraid, and will be at peace [*afterward.*] But though he be impudent, and insist in his malice yet even in that case do thou forgive him, from thine heart, and leave vengeance to God.

Luk. xvi. 3, 4.

Deut. xxxii. 35. Ps. xciv. 1. Heb. x. 30.

§. 7. If any one be prospered more than You be ye not troubled; but pray for him, that he may be completely prospered. For perhaps this is for your good; nay, though he should be greatly exalted, do not envy him: remembering that all flesh shall die. But offer an hymn of praise to the Lord, who giveth what is good and profitable unto all Men. Search out the judgments of the Lord; and so will he forgive thee, and will make thy mind peaceable. Nay, if any of the wicked grows rich, as was the case of *Esau*, my father's brother, do not ye envy him; but wait for the appointed time of the Lord. For either He will take them away by misfortunes; or will forgive them upon repentance; or if such an one he impenitent, he will reserve his punishment for the future world. He that is needy, and without envy, giving thank always to the Lord, he is richer than they all: because he hath not the evil distraction of Men. Take therefore hatred away from your Souls, and love one another in uprightness of heart.

§. 8. But do you your selves, tell this to your Sons; that they are to honour *Judas*, and *Levi*. For out of them, the Lord will arise to you, a Saviour to *Israel*. For I know that in the end, your Sons will depart from them, and will be immersed in all wickedness, and affliction, and corruption before the Lord. And when he had rested himself again, he said to them, My Sons, Hear your father; and bury me near my fathers. And plucking up his feet, he slept in peace. And after five years, they brought him back to *Hebron*, and buried him there with his fathers.

A S E R.

A copy of the Testament of *Aser*, which he spake to his Sons, in the 126th year of his life: while he was in health: He said unto them, Hear, Ye Sons of *Aser*, your father: and I will shew You whatsoever is right in the sight of God. God hath set *Two Ways* before the Sons of Men: two courses of life; and two sorts of practice; and two places; and two ends. Wherefore all things are two, the one set over against the other. Two ways of good and of evil: as to which, there are two Counsels within our breasts, that

Deut. xxx. 15, 19. See Constitut. VII. 1. &c. Barnab. §. 18. &c. Her.Mand. VI. 1.

distinguish them. If therefore the Soul be inclined to what is good, all, its practice is in righteousness: if he sin, he presently repents. For by intending to do what is right, and by casting away wickedness, he soon overturns what is evil, and cuts up sin by the roots. But if the Soul's inclination be to do what is evil, its actions partake of wickedness; and by the rejection of what is good, he embraces what is evil; and being over-ruled by *Beliar*, although he does some what that is good, he converts it to wickedness: for tho he begins as intending to do good, yet is the conclusion of His actions perverted, and turned to do evil: because the treasure of the understanding is filled with the poison of a wicked Spirit.

§. 2. There is a Soul that speaks and says, that good is better than evil; and yet it conducts the end of the action to evil. There is a Man that has no compassion upon him, that ministered to him in doing mischief. This also has two faces; but the whole of it is wicked. There is also a Man that loves one that is acting wickedly; who is in like manner in Wickedness, for that he chooses to die in acting what is evil on his account. Now as to this also, it is manifest that the thing has two faces; but the whole of it is wicked practice. And though the thing be love, yet it is wickedness, and it obscures what is good: accordingly, it has a good name, but the end of the action comes to evil. Another Man steals, acts unjustly, takes things away by force, is greedy of more; yet hath he mercy on the poor. Now truly this has also two faces; but the whole is wicked. He that greedily gets his neighbour's goods, provokes

God to anger, and adjures the Most High to a falsehood: yet hath he mercy on the poor: He rejects him that is the teacher of the Law of the Lord, yet. does he refresh the needy: He defiles the Soul, but amends the Body: He kills many, but hath mercy on a few. This also hath two faces. Another is guilty of adultery and fornication, yet he abstains from food: and as he fasteth he ads wickedness: and by his power and his riches he vexes many; and out of his arrogant wickedness performs the [*other*] commands. This also hath two faces; but the whole of it is wicked. Such persons are like swine and hares, who as to one half of their character, are clean; but in reality are unclean. For so did the Lord say in the *Tables of the Heavens*.

Levit. xi. 6, 7. Deut. xiv. 7, 8.

§. 3. Be not you therefore, My Sons like these Men of two faces, the one of goodness, the other of wickedness; but do you adhere only to goodness. For God acquiesces therein and that is it which Men desire. But fly from wickedness, and get clear of the Devil; by your good works: for those that have two faces do not serve God; but their Own lusts; that they may please *Beliar* and such Men as are like him.

§. 4. For good Men, and those that have but one face, though they appear to such as have two faces to sin, are righteous with God. For many who destroy the wicked do two works, a good work by an evil one: but the whole is good: for by rooting out wickedness it perishes. One hateth a merciful Man, and accuses him as an adulterer and a thief. This also hath two faces; but the whole work is good; because he imitates the Lord; in not receiving that which appeals to be good, together with what is really evil. Another will not see a good day with extravagant persons, that he may not defile his Body, and pollute his Soul. This also hath two faces; but the whole is good. For such as these are like to goats stags who under a wild behaviour seem to be unclean, but upon the whole are clean.: for they walk in the zeal of God, abstaining from those things which God hatcth, and by his precepts forbids; separating evil from good.

Deut. xiv. 4, 5.

§. 5. See, My Sons, how every thing is double, and one thing is obscured by another. Death succeeds to life; dishonour to honour; night to day; light to darkness: but all things are under the day. Righteous actions are under life: wherefore eternal life waits us after death; nor is it lawful to call truth falsehood, nor justice injustice: for all truth is under the light; as all things are under God. I have had experience of all this in my life: and I have not gone astray from the truth of the Lord: and I have sought out the commands of the Most High: and according to my entire ability, have I walked with one face to do good.

§. 6. Do you therefore, My Sons, attend to the commands of the Lord: following truth with one face: for those that have two faces, shall be doubly punished; as imitating the Spirits of Error, which strive against Men. Keep the Law of the Lord; and do not attend to evil as to good: but have regard to what is really good; and observe that, in all the commands of the Lord: returning unto him, and resting finally in him: (for the ends of Men shew their Righteousness.)

And do you acquaint you your selves with the Angels of the Lord, and the Angels of Satan: for when a Soul goes away disordered, it is tormented by the wicked Spirit, to which it was a servant in lusts, and wicked works; but if in silence and gladness, it be acquainted with the Angel, of peace, he will comfort him in life.

§. 7. Be not ye like to *Sodom*: which knew not the Angels of the Lord, and perished for ever. *Gen. xix.* For I know that ye will sin, and will be delivered into the hand of your enemies; your land will be made desolate: and you will be scattered abroad, unto the four corners of the earth: and you will be in a dispersion, utterly despised as useless water; until the Most High shall visit the Earth, and he himself shall come, as a Man, eating and drinking with Men: and in silence bruising the head of the dragon by water. He shall save *Israel* and all the Gentiles, being a God putting on the appearance of a Man. Tell ye therefore this to your children, that they be not disobedient to him. For I have read In the *Tables of the Heavens*, that you will certainly disobey him, and you will certainly act wickedly towards him: not attending to the Law of God, but to the commandments of Men. For this, cause shall ye be scattered abroad, as shall *Gad* and *Dan* [*and the rest of*] my brethren: who shall not know their own countries or their own tribe, or language. But the Lord will gather you together in faith, by the hope of his compassion: for the sake of *Abraham*, and *Isaac* and *Jacob*.

§. 8. And having said this to them, he charged them, saying, Bury me in *Hebron*. And he died, sleeping a good sleep. And his Sons did according to what he charged them: and they brought him back, and buried him with his fathers.

JOSEPH.

A copy of the Testament of *Joseph*. When he was about to die, he called his Sons and his Brethren, and said unto them, My Sons, and Brethren, Hear *Joseph*, the beloved of *Israel*. Hearken, My Sons, to your Father. I have seen in my life envy and death: and I did not err in the truth of the Lord. These brethren of mine hated me, and the Lord loved me: they would have killed me, but the Lord of my fathers preserved me: they let me down into a pit, and the Most High brought me up again: I was sold for a servant, and God made me free: I was taken as a captive, and his strong hand helped me: I was *distressed by famine, and the Lord himself nourished me: I was in weakness, and the Most High visited me: I was in prison, and my Saviour dealt graciously with me: in bonds, and he loosed me: under false accusations, and he pleaded for me: under bitter words of the *Egyptians* and he delivered me: under envy and deceit, and he exalted me.

§. 2. And accordingly, *Photimar*, [*Potiphar*] *the Captain of *Pharaoh*'s guard committed his house to me: and I was in an agony about his wife, an impudent woman, who solicited me to transgress with her. But the God of *Israel*, my father, preserved me out of the burning flame. I was put into prison, I was beaten with stripes, I was affronted with scorn; and the Lord made me

In the pit Zabul. §. 4. Matt. xxv. 45, 36.

* Αρχιμά-γεϸοϛ. *Vid. Hieron Trad. Heb. in Gen. xxxvii. 36.*

an object of compassion in the sight of the Keeper of the prison. For the Lord will not leave those that fear him, neither in darkness, nor in bonds, nor in adversities, nor in distress. For God is not ashamed of them as Man is: nor is he afraid as the Son of Man is; nor is he weak, or easily repulsed, as is he that is born upon Earth. But he is present in all places, and comforts Men in different marnners; though he some times leaves them for a while, to try the disposition of their Soul. He has made me an example of such trial in ten temptations; and I Exercised long-suffering in them all: for long-suffering is a great remedy, and patience bestows many blessings.

§. 3. How often did the *Egyptian* woman threaten me with death? How often did she recall me from the punishment she had denounced against me, and threatened me when I would not lie with her? And she said, Thou shalt rule over me, and over all that is mine, if thou wilt give up thy self to me: and thou shalt be as our master. I therefore called to mind the words of the fathers of my father *Jacob*, [*Abraham, and Isaac*,] and *entering into my closet, I prayed* to the Lord, and I fasted in those seven years, and I appeared to the *Egyptian* [*Potiphar*} as if I had lived delicately. For those that fast for God's sake, receive the grace of the countenance; [*are well-favoured.*] And when wine was given me, I did not drink of it: and when I fasted three days together, I received my provision, and gave it to the poor, and to the infirm, I got up early to pray to the Lord; and I wept on account of this *Egyptian* woman of *Memphis*. For she was troublesome to me, without the least

Matt. vi. 6.

Dan. i. 10——15.

intermission. And in the night time she would come to me, on pretense of visiting me. And at first she pretended that she had no male issue, and made me believe she esteemed me as her own Son. And I prayed unto the Lord, and she bare a Son. For some time she embraced me as a Son: and I understood not [*her meaning.*] At last she tempted me to fornication and when I understood it, I was sorrowful, even unto death and when she was gone out, I came to myself, and I was grieved for her many days: and I spake to her the words of the Most High, if perhaps she might be converted from her wicked lust.

§. **4.** How often did she flatter me, as if I were an holy man: commending my chastity treacherously in words, before her husband; while she was desirous to supplant me when I was alone? She boasted of me publickly, as of a chaste person; but in private she said to me, Be not afraid of my husband: for he is persuaded of thy chastity: so that if any one should tell him of us, he will not believe it. On this account I prostrated myself on the ground; and besought God that he would deliver me from this *Egyptian* woman. But when she could not prevail, she came again to me for instruction in religion; to learn the word of the Lord; and she said to me, If thou art desirous that I should leave Idols, yield to me, and I will persuade this *Egyptian* to leave his Idols, and we will walk in the Law of thy Lord. I said to her, The Lord does not desire that His worshippers should do it in uncleanness nor has he pleasure in fornicators. Upon which she was silent; but desirous to fulfill her lust. I also still the more fasted and prayed, that the Lord would deliver me from her.

§. 5. Again, at another time she said to me, If thou wilt not commit fornication, I will slay this *Egyptian;* and then I will take thee for my husband, according to law. Whereupon, as soon as I heard this, I rent my garment, and said, Woman, fear the Lord; and do not perpetrate so wicked a thing, lest thou be destroyed, For even I myself will tell thy wicked purpose to all men. Upon which she prayed that I would not declare her wickedness to any: and she went away, seducing me still with presents, and sending me all the rarities the Sons of Men do enjoy.

§. 6. She also sent me meat, mixed by art-magick: and as the Eunuch came and brought it to me, I looked up, and saw a terrible man giving me a sword, together with the dish and I understood that this pernicious practice was for the misleading of my Soul and when he was gone out, I wept, but did not taste either that meat, or any other that she sent me. Now. one day after this, when she came to me, she perceived the meat was there still; and she said to me, What is the matter that thou hast not eaten of this meat? And I said to her, Thou hast filled it with what is deadly. And how canst thou say I do not come near to idols, but to the Lord only? Know therefore now, that the God of my father, by his Angel, hath revealed to me thy wickedness: and I kept this meat for thy conviction, if possibly, by seeing it, thou mayest repent. Now, that thou mayest learn, that the mischief of the impious does not prevail over those that worship God with purity, I took it before her face, and did eat; and said, The God of my fathers, and the Angel of *Abraham* will be with me. Whereupon she fell upon her face, at my feet, and wept; and when I had taken her up, I instructed her, and she promised that she would no more ad such impiety.

§. 7. But her heart was still set upon me, for adultery: she groaned, and had a dejected countenance. And the *Egyptian* [*her husband*] said to her, why is thy countenance dejected? And she said, I am troubled at heart, and the groans of my Spirit oppress me. And he endeavoured to cure her that was not sick. Then she came running to me, when her husband was abroad, and said to me, I will hang myself, or throw myself into a pit, or down a precipice, unless thou wilt agree to my proposal. And when I perceived that the Spirit or *Beliar* disturbed her, I prayed to the Lord; and said to her, why art thou troubled, and in disorder, and blinded in sins? Remember that if thou kill thy self, *Sethon* thy husband's concubine, thy rival, will box thy children, and will destroy thy memorial out of the Earth. And she said to me, me, if then thou lovest me, I am satisfied with this alone, that thou valuest my life, and the life of my children; and I cannot but expect [*at length*] to obtain my desire. And she knew not that it was on the account of the Lord, that I said this, and not on her account: for if any one be subject to the passion of a wicked lust, and be enslaved thereto, as this woman was, though such an one hear any good thing, it is taken as subordinate to that passion, by which the party is overcome; and in order to gain their wicked desire.

§. 8. I tell you therefore, My Sons, that it was about the sixth hour when she went out from me; when I bended my knee to the Lord, joining together that whole day, and that whole night, and in the morning I got up weeping, and begging deliverance from this *Egyptian* Woman. At last, she caught hold, of my garments, forcibly, drawing me to accompany with her. As soon therefore, as I saw that she was so mad as to take hold of my garments, I fled away naked; and she accused me falsely to her husband: and the *Egyptian* cast me into prison, in his own house: and the next day, when he had chastised me with stripes, he sent me into *Pharaoh's* prison, As soon then as I was in bonds, the *Egyptian* Woman was sick with grief, and hearkened how I sung hymns to the Lord, in the house of darkness: and rejoicing with a cheerful voice, I alone glorified God, that by this means, I was got free of the *Egyptian* Woman.

§. 9. Yet did she frequently send to me, saying, Be but willing to fulfil my desire, and I will redeem thee from thy bonds; and I will deliver thee from thy darkness. And I did not yield to her inclinations, no not in my thoughts. For God rather loves one that is in a dark prison, if he fast in chastity; than one in royal chambers, that lives deliciously with impurity. But if he who lives in chastity, desires also glory; and if the Most High see it be for his advantage, He also bestows that upon him: as he did upon me. How often did the Woman, when she was ill, come down to me in my dark place, and heard my voice when I was praying? But when I perceived her groans, I kept silent: for even when I was in her house, she would shew me her bare arms, her breast, and her legs, that I might fall into her snares: for she Was exceeding beautiful; especially, when she adorned her self to deceive me. But the Lord preserved me from her attempts.

§. **10.** Consider therefore, My Sons, what efficacy there is in patience, and prayer, with fasting. Even if you your selves obtain chastity and purity, in patience and humility of heart, the Lord will dwell in you: for he loveth chastity. Now where the Most High dwelleth, although any one fall under envy, or slavery, or false accusation, or darkness, the Lord who dwelleth in him, on account of his chastity, will not only deliver him out of his afflictions, but will also exalt him, and bring him to glory; as he did me. For it must needs be, that a Man is distressed, either in deed, or in word, or in thought. My brethren know how well my father loved me, and yet I was not exalted in my mind; although I were but young, yet had I the fear of God in my heart; for I knew that all things will pass away: and I did not exceed my bounds: and I honoured my brethren: and out of regard to them I kept silence, when I was sold; so that I did not tell my parentage to the Ishmaelites, that I was the Son of *Jacob*, a man of great power and authority.

§. **11.** Do you therefore retain, in all actions, the fear of God before your eyes; and honour your brethren: for every one that does the law of the Lord, shall be beloved by him. When therefore I came to. the *Indicolpitae*, with the *Ishmaelites*, they asked me, and I said, I am an household servant: that I might not disgrace my brethren. Now the chief of them said to me, Thou art not a servant: for even thy countenance shews what thou art: and he threatened me even to death. But I still said, I am their servant. Now as soon as we came into *Egypt*, they strove about me, who should purchase me; for it was supposed by every body, that I was in *Egypt* with their factor, only until they should return with their merchandize. And the Lord gave me favour in the eyes of the factor; and he trusted me with his house: and God blessed, him by my hand, and increased him with silver and gold and I was with him three months and five days.

§. 12. At that time the woman of *Memphis*, the wife of *Potiphar*, passed by, in great pomp: and she cast her eyes upon me. For her Eunuchs told her of me. And she spake to her husband about the factor, that he was grown rich by the means of a certain youth of the *Hebrews*: and they said, that for certain they had stolen him out of the land of *Canaan*. Therefore now do him justice: and take away this youth that he may be thy Steward; and the God of the *Hebrews* will bless thee: for favour from heaven is upon him.

§. 13. Now *Potiphar* was persuaded by her words, and commanded the factor to be brought to him: and he said to him, How is it that I hear this of thee, that thou stealest Men out of the land of the *Hebrews*, and sellest them for servants? Whereupon the factor fell upon his face, and made supplication, and said, Have mercy on me, My Lord: I know not what thou sayest. And he said, Whence then didst thou get this Hebrew Servant? And he said, The *Ishmaelites* committed him to my care, until their return. But he did not believe him; but commanded him to be stripped and scourged, But when he continued in the same story, *Potiphar* said, Let the youth be brought hither. And when he was brought, he bowed down before the master of the Eunuchs: for he was the third in dignity in *Pharaoh*'s court; the Prince of all the Eunuchs: having wives, and concubines, and children. And when he had taken me aside, he said, Art thou a slave, or a freeman? And I said, A slave. And he said to me, Whose slave art thou? And I said to them, The *Ishmaelites* slave. And again he said to me, How didst .thou become their Slave? And I said, They bought me out of the land of *Canaan*. But he did not believe me, saying, Thou certainly tellest a lie. And he commanded me to be stripped and scourged.

§. **14.** Now the woman of *Memphis* saw me through her window, as I was scourging: and she sent to her husband, saying, This is an unjust sentence; for thee to punish a free man that has been stolen away, without any crime of his. But since I did not change my story upon scourging, he commanded that we should be kept, until, as he said, the masters of this servant shall come. And his wife said to him, Why dost thou imprison a captive, one of good parentage; one who should rather be let go, and minister to thee? (for she was desirous to see me, with an inclination to sin: while I was entirely ignorant of all this.) But he said to this woman of *Memphis*, It is not lawful, among the *Egyptians*, before Men are convicted, to take away what belongs to others. He said this as to the factor:

and that the slave ought to be kept in safe custody.

§. **15.** Now after 24 days, came the *Ishmaelites* and having heard that *Jacob* my father lamented for me, they said to me, wherefore didst thou say of myself, I am a Slave: and lo we know that thou art the Son of a great Man, in the land of *Canaan;* and thy father lamenteth for thee in sackcloth. Upon which I had a great inclination to weep: but I refrained myself, that I might not disgrace my brethren. And I said, I know nothing of that, I am a slave. They then resolved to sell me, that I might not be found in their hands: for they were afraid of *Jacob,* lest he should take vengeance on them, for bringing me into peril. For they heard that he was great both with God and Men. Then said the factor to them, Get him loosed from the sentence of *Potiphar.* They then came to me, and desired a favour of me, saying, Tell [*Potiphar,*] that thou wast bought by us with money, and he will loose thee.

§. **16.** Now the woman of *Memphis,* made known her mind to her husband, that she desired him to purchase me: for, says she, I hear that they will sell him. And she sent an Eunuch to the *Ishmaelites,* desiring to purchase me. [*Upon which, the Captain of the guard asked the Ishmaelites to buy me.*] And the Eunuch upon trial, was unwilling to bargain with them, and went his way: but told his mistress, that they asked a great price for the servant. Upon which she sent another Eunuch, and said, Though they should even ask two pounds of gold, give it. Spare not for gold: only buy the servant and bring him. And he gave 80 pieces of gold for me; telling the

Egyptian woman, that he had given an 100 for me. However, though I saw this, I said nothing that the Eunuch might not be called to an account.

§. **17.** Consider, My Sons how much I endured, that I might not disgrace my brethren. Do you therefore also love one another; and with long-suffering, conceal one another's imperfections. God is pleased with the concord of brethren; and that disposition of heart, which is well inclined to love. Moreover, when my brethren came into *Egypt*, they know that I returned their money, and did not reproach them; but even comforted them: and after the death of *Jacob*, I loved them more abundantly; and whatsoever he enjoined me, I did it, over and above, till they wondered at it. For I did not permit them to be distressed in the least thing. I also bestowed on them, whatsoever was in my power: their Sons, were my Sons and my Sons, were as servants to them. Their Soul, was my Soul: and all their grief, was my grief, and all their sickness, was my infirmity; my land, was their land: my Counsel, was their counsel: nor did I arrogantly exalt myself among them, on account of my worldly glory. But I was among them, as one of the least of them.

§. **18.** If therefore you also will walk in the commandments of the Lord, My Sons, He will advance you, and will bless you with good things for ever. And if any one would do you mischief, out of your good will to him, pray for him; and you shall be delivered from all evil by the Lord. For behold now, you see, that on account of my long-suffering I was permitted to marry the daughter of my master and mistress; and 100 talents of gold were given me with her: for God made them my servants. He also gave me beauty like a flower above the beautiful ones of *Israel*; and he kept me unto old age in strength and beauty: for I was in all things like unto *Jacob*.

§. 19. But now, My Sons, Hear the dream which I saw Twelve stags were feeding, and nine of them were divided from the rest, and were dispersed over all the Earth. In like manner were the three. And I saw that a Virgin was born of *Judah* that had on a fine linen garment: and from her proceeded a spotless Lamb: and on its left hand there was a Lion; and all the wild beasts ran against him, and the Lamb overcame them, and destroyed them; till they were utterly trodden down. And in him did Angels, and Men, and all the Earth rejoice. Now these things shall be fulfilled in their season, in the last days. Do you therefore, My Sons, keep the commandments of the Lord; and honour *Judah* and *Levi*: for out of them shall arise to you the Lamb of God by grace saving all the Gentiles, and *Israel* also. For his Kingdom will be an eternal Kingdom, which shall not be moved. But my Kingdom among you will have an end, as a garden of fruit; for after summer is over, it will appear no more.

§. 20. I know that after my decease the *Egyptians* will afflict you: but God will avenge you; and will bring you into the land promised to your fathers. But you shall carry my bones along with you: for if my bones be carried back, the Lord will be in the light with you; and *Beliar* in darkness with the *Egyptians*. Do you also [*Gad*

2 ½.
2 Bar. i.
Præs.
4 Esd. xiii.
40 Arab.

Apoc.
XVII. 14.

and Aser} carry back *Zilpha,* your mother; and lay her near *Bilha*h, at the *Hippodrome,* hard by *Rachel.* And when he had said this, he stretched out his feet, and slept the eternal sleep. And all *Israel,* and all *Egypt* mourned for him, a great mourning. For he had compassion on the *Egyptians,* as his own members: and did them good; assisting them in every work, and Counsel, and thing whatsoever.

BENJAMIN.

A copy of the words of Benjamin which he spake, as his Testament, to his Sons, when he had lived 125 years. And he kissed them, and said, As *Isaac* was born to *Abraham* in his hundredth year, so was I to *Jacob*. And because *Rachel* died as soon as she had born me, I could not suck her milk: but I sucked of *Bilhah*. For *Rachel*, after she had brought forth *Joseph*, was barren twelve years; and she prayed to the Lord with fasting twelve days; and she conceived and bare me. For our father loved *Rachel* exceedingly; and prayed that he might have two Sons born of her. For this cause her Son was called *the Son of Days*, which is the signification of Benjamin, [*or Benjamim.*] *Gen. xxxv. 18.*

§. 2. When therefore I went into *Egypt*, and *Joseph* my brother took notice of me, he said to me, What did they say to my father when they had sold me? And I said to him, they dipped thy coat in blood; and sending it to him, they said, Consider whether this be thy Son's coat. And he said to me, 'Tis true, Brother, for when the *Ishmaelites* took me, one of them plucked off my coat, and gave me a girdle, and when he had given me a lash with his whip, he bid me run. But as he went to hide my coat, a lion met him, and slew him. Upon which his partners were affrighted, and sold me to their companions.

§. 3. Do you also, therefore, My Sons, your selves love the God of Heaven, and keep his commandments; in imitation of that good and holy man *Joseph*: and let your mind be set upon that which is good; as you. see my mind has been. He that hath a good mind sees every thing rightly. fear the Lord, and love your neighbour: and if the Spirits of *Beliar* shall desire to have you led into all the wickedness of affliction, [*temptations of adversity*,] all that wickedness of affliction shall not have dominion over you; as neither had it dominion over *Joseph*, my brother. How many men had a mind to kill him? and God protected him: for he that fears God, and loves his neighbour, cannot be subject to the strokes of the aerial Spirit of *Beliar*; being covered by the fear of God: and he cannot be overcome by the snares of men, or of beasts; being afflicted by that love of the Lord which he bears towards his neighbour. For he desired of our father *Jacob* that he would pray for our brethren, that the Lord would not impute it to them that they had wickedly contrived his ruin. Whereupon *Jacob* cried out, O my good Son *Joseph*! thou hast overcome the bowels of *Jacob* thy, father. And embracing him, he kissed him for two Hours together, saying, The prophecy of Heaven concerning the *Lamb of God*, and *Saviour of the World*, shall be fulfilled in thee: for the spotless one shall delivered Up for transgressors, and the sinless one shall die for the impious, in the blood of the covenant, for the salvation of *Israel*, and of all the Gentiles: and he shall destroy *Beliar*, and those that minister unto him.

Test. Jos. §. 19. Test. Dan. §. 6.

§. 4. You have seen, My Sons, the end of that good man. Imitate therefore, with a good mind, his compassion; that you also may wear crowns of glory. A good man hath not a dark eye: for he hath mercy upon all: although they be sinners, although they contrive his ruin. Such an one, by doing good, conquers the evil one; and is protected by the Good Being. He loves righteous men, as his own Soul. If any one becomes glorious, he does not envy him. If any one grows rich, he is not jealous of him. If any one be valiant, he commends him. If he believes a Man to be chaste, he praises him. He shews mercy to him that is poor: he is compassionate to him that is infirm: he sings praises to God. He protects him that hath the fear of God. He helps the man that loves God. He admonishes and converts him that despises the Most High: and he loves, as his Soul, the Man that hath the happiness of a good Spirit.

§. 5. If therefore you have a good mind, My Sons, both wicked men will be at peace with you; and prodigals will have a reverence for you, and will be converted to What is good; and covetous men will not only leave off that passion, but will give what their covetousness hath gained to those that are afflicted. If you do good, even the unclean Spirits will fly from you; and the wild beasts themselves will be afraid of you: for where the light of good works is in the mind, darkness flies away thence. For if any one deals unjustly with an holy Man, he repents of it: for the holy Man is merciful to him that reproaches him, and is silent: and though any one should betray a righteous man, and the righteous Man who prays for him, is for a while humbled, yet does he in a little time appear more glorious: as happened in the instance of *Joseph* my brother.

§. 6. The mind of a good man is not under the power of the seduction of the Spirit of *Beliar*: for the Angel of peace conducts his Soul. He has not a passionate regard to things corruptible: nor does he collect riches for the love of pleasure: he is not delighted [*too much*] with pleasure: he does not grieve his neighbour: he does not fill himself with delicacies: he does not wander about with lofty eyes: for the Lord is his portion. A good mind does not admit of the glory and disgrace of men: it hath no knowledge of deceit, or lying, of war, or reproach: for the Lord dwells therein, and illuminates his Soul, and he rejoices towards all Men, and at all times. A good mind hath not two tongues, of blessing and of cursing; of injury and of honour; of quiet and of disturbance; of hypocrisy and of truth; of poverty and of riches: but it hath towards all Men a sincere and pure disposition. It has neither the light, nor the hearing double: for whatever it either does, or says, or sees, it knows that the Lord looks upon his Soul; and he purifies his understanding, that he may not be condemned by God or Men. Every work of *Beliar* is also double, and hath no simplicity in it.

§. 7. Wherefore, My Sons, flee from the wickedness of *Beliar*: for it does but bring a sword upon those that are subject thereto. And this sword is the mother of seven evils, which the mind first conceives by *Beliar*: when it afterwards bears, first envy; secondly destruction; thirdly affliction; fourthly captivity; fifthly want; sixthly trouble; seventhly desolation. On which account also, *Cain* was delivered over to seven punishments: for at the

Jam. i. 15.

Gen. iv. 15.

125

end of every hundred years, the Lord inflicted a stroke upon him. He was 200 years old, when his sufferings began: and he was made desolate [*suffered,*] in the 900th year of his life, on account of Abel his righteous brother. In seven hundred years, [*or seven periods*] was *Cain* judged: but Lamech in seventy times seven. For those which are like to *Cain*, in such sort of envy as produces hatred of our brethren, shall for ever be condemned to the same punishment.

See Suppl. to Lit. Ac- compl. Of Script. Pro. p. 106—132.

§. 8. Do you therefore, My Sons, flee from wickedness, envy, and hatred of your brethren: and adhere to goodness, and love; He that hath a pure mind in love, he does not look on a Woman for fornication: for he has no pollution in his heart: for the Spirit of God rests upon him. For as the Sun is not polluted, when it shines upon dung or ditches; but rather dries up both, and drives away their ill favour: so does a pure mind, that is confined within the polluted places of the Earth, rather edify them; without any defilement by them.

§. 9. I understand also, that there will be practices that are not good among you, from the words of *Enoch* the Righteous. For you will be guilty of such fornication, as was in *Sodom*; and you will be very near to destruction; and you will renew your selves by women of luxury; and the Kingdom of the Lord, shall not be [*long*] among you: for he will himself soon take it. However, the Temple of God shall be in your portion, and will be glorious among [*above the first.*] For he will himself soon; take it: and the twelve tribes, shall be gathered thither and all the Gentiles: until the Most High send his

Judg. xix, xx, xxi.

N.B. The Temple of Solomon, rebuilt by Zorobabel, Nehemiah, salvation, by the visitation of the Only begotten, [*Prophet.*] And he shall enter into the *first Temple*: and there the Lord shall suffer injuries; and shall be lift up upon a Tree; and the veil of the Temple shall be rent; and the Spirit of God, shall remove to the Gentiles, as fire poured out upon them. And when he has come up, out of the invisible world, he shall ascend from Earth to Heaven. Now I know how he will be in a low estate up on Earth; and how he will be in a glorious second estate in Heaven.

Solomon II. and Herod, on mount Moriah, was the first Temple, Hag. ii. 9. As that to be hereafter built on mt. Sion, will be the second

§. 10. Now when *Joseph* was in *Egypt*, I was desirous to see his image, and the form of his countenance: and through the prayers of my father *Jacob* I saw him, as I was awake, in the day time; exactly according to his image. Know ye therefore, My Sons, that I am ready to die. Do ye therefore truth and Righteousness, every one with his neighbour; with justice and assured fidelity: and keep ye the Law of the Lord, and his commandments: for this is what I teach you, instead of [*leaving you*] all other kinds of inheritance. Do you therefore also deliver this to your children, for an eternal possession. For this did *Abraham*, and *Isaac*, and *Jacob*: they gave you all these, instructions for an inheritance, and said, *Keep ye the commandments of God; until the time when the Lord shall reveal his salvation to all the Gentiles.* Then shall ye see *Enoch*, and Noah, and Sem, and *Abraham*, and *Isaac*, and *Jacob*, risen from the dead, at his right hand, in exultation. Then shall we also rise again, ever one upon our scepter adorning the King of the Heavens, who had appeared upon Earth in the form of man's humiliation: and as many as have believed him

Gen. xviii. 17, 18, 19.

upon Earth, shall rejoice together with him: at which time *all men shall rise again, some to, glory, and others to disgrace*: and the Lord will judge *Israel* in the first; place, and on account of their injustice; that they did not believe in God when be came as their deliverer in the flesh. And then he will judge all the Gentiles, as many as have not believed in him, when he appeared upon Earth: and he will reprove *Israel* by his elect among the Gentiles; as he reproved *Esau* among the Midianites, who had seduced him to become their brother, by fornication and idolatry; and they were alienated from God. Do you therefore, My Sons, continue in the portion of those that fear the Lord. Now if you shall walk in sanctification before the face of the Lord, you shall again dwell with assurance in me; and *Israel* shall be gathered together to the Lord. *Dan. xii. 2.*

Ps. 1.

Test. Jud. §. 9.

§. 11. Moreover, I shall no longer be called a *ravening wolf*, on account of your ravages: but the Lord's labourer distributing food to those that work what is good. And one beloved of the Lord shall be raised up out of thy Seed, in the last days; One that shall hear his voice, and do the good pleasure of his will, and illuminate all the Gentiles with new Knowledge, the light of knowledge in the salvation of *Israel*: like a wolf snatching it from him, and giving it to the congregation of the Gentiles: and until the consummation of the ages, he shall be among the congregations of the Gentiles, and among their rulers, as a musical song in the mouth of all. And he have his name written in the Holy Books; as also his work, and his doctrine: and he shall be the cleft of God for ever. And on his *Gen. xlix. 27. Sept.*

Paul the Apostle.

Acts of the Apostles, Paul's Epistles.

account it was that *Jacob* my father instructed me, saying, He shall fill up the defects of thy tribe: [*i.e. in his early age he shall be a devourer of the prey: in his last age a divider of the food of the Jews among the Gentiles.*]

Gen. xlix. 27. Sept.

§. 12. And as soon as he had finished his words, he said, I charge you, My Sons, carry back my bones out of *Egypt,* and bury me in *Hebron* near my fathers. And Benjamin died 125 years old, in a good old age: and they put him in a coffin. And in the 90th year *before the coming of the children of *Israel* out of *Egypt,* they and their brethren brought back the bones of their fathers, privately, in the [*Egyptian*] war, unto *Canaan*; and they buried them in *Hebron*, at the feet of their fathers. And they returned out of the land of *Canaan*, and dwelt in *Egypt*, until the day of their Exodus out of the land of *Egypt*.

* after gr.

Test. Symeon §. 8.

The End of the XII Testaments *of the* Sons *of* Jacob.

Appendix to the 21ˢᵗ Century Edition:
Enoch Concealed. Enoch Revealed.

In William Whiston's *Extracts out of the First Book of Enoch, Concerning the Egregori: [or fallen Angels]* we have the early rumblings of what was to become the long modern process by which the *Book of Enoch* would come out of its long hiatus away from the attention of the world.

In a 2020 article[1], Colby Townsend fully documents all the literature which was available in English concerning the *Book of Enoch*, before 1821. Among other things, his research shows that Whiston was the first to affirm that *Enoch*'s book should be accepted as a legitimate part of the Bible.

It would be fifty years after Whiston published his thoughts on *Enoch*, that James Bruce would bring back from Ethiopia the first complete copies of the text of *Enoch*. It would be another fifty years before any complete translation of *Enoch* would become available to English readers.

The Life of Enoch as Parable

In the *Book of Enoch* itself, we discover how the process of concealing and revealing was played out in the life of *Enoch* as well…

> Before these things *Enoch* was hidden, and no one of the children of men knew where he was hidden, and where he abode, and what had become of him. And his activities had to do with the Watchers, and his days were with the holy ones. And I *Enoch* was

---

[1] Townsend, Colby. "Revisiting *Joseph* Smith and the Availability of the Book of Enoch." Dialogue: A Journal of Mormon Thought, vol. 53, no. 3, 2020, pp. 41-72.

blessing the Lord of majesty and the King of the ages, and lo! the Watchers called me -*Enoch* the scribe- and said to me: '*Enoch*, thou scribe of righteousness, go, declare to the Watchers...

(*Enoch* 12:1-4 Charles)

In the above passage, before being called to ministry, and before his translation, *Enoch* had been *hidden away* from mankind, spending time worshiping God with the heavenly host. *Enoch* was *hidden away* and after some time he received his call to preach God's message. During the days of his earthly sojourn, *Enoch*, the man, entered into the purpose for his life's calling after returning from his days in seclusion.

When this happened, *Enoch* was living out as if in parable what would be the future status of the book he wrote. *Enoch*'s book, like *Enoch*, has been hidden for a time, and now is gradually coming into the spotlight for which it was purposed when written. *Enoch* hinted at this possibility when he said the book he wrote so long ago was *"not for this generation, but for a remote one which is for to come"* and for, *"the righteous, who will be living in the day of tribulation"*. (*Enoch* 1:1-2)

Like *Enoch*, the book he wrote has gone through a period of seclusion, or *sequestration*, if you will. In this way, *Enoch*'s book has become a kind of time-capsule, dramatically appearing on the scene which is exactly what is happening in our time.

The *Book of Enoch* has passed through a number of phases in its process of being concealed and revealed on the world scene.

Rejected by official Judaism

This first phase occurred shortly after the ministry of Christ and the Apostles. The *Book of Enoch* had been in wide circulation leading up to this period. It was evidently widely popular, even being viewed as holy scripture and quoted in many other books of the day. However, in the late first century, the spiritual leadership of the Jews of the day, decided upon a strict canon of scripture, one which eliminated a number of books, including *Enoch*, as well as the writings of the Apostles.

Banned by Churchmen and Clerics

The *Book of Enoch* continued for a time to be popular among early Christian writers and in the churches. *Enoch's* book is referred to in a positive manner in the writings of *Irenaeus*, Clement, Tertullian, Athenagoras, Tatian, Lactantius, Methodius, Minucius Felix, Commodianus and Ambrose, being often treated as holy scripture. Gradually however, *Enoch's* popularity dimmed within Christianity. As Greek ideas about the nature of angels began to permeate Christian thought, the book fell into disfavor. The book was forbidden by the Council of Laodicea in the late 4th century A.D. Apparently, Augustine was influential in further pushing the book into obscurity. Ultimately, the *Book of Enoch* was removed from the libraries of the churches of the Mediterranean world.

Concealed & Preserved in Africa

The sequestration of the *Book of Enoch* was fully underway by the fifth century A.D. The book had passed from being widely available into a state wherein its pages were not allowed read in the churches, neither were its pages thought worthy of being copied and preserved. The book passed into a time in which *no one of the children of men* in the Greek and Latin worlds knew *where it was hidden, and where it abode, and what had become of it.* However, its hiding was for a purpose. Like Jesus' flight to *Egypt*, *Enoch's* book was being preserved for the mission for which it had been purposed from the first. From the outset, the *Book of Enoch* was destined to return from its hidden period to center stage for the benefit of a *remote generation which was for to come.* Just as first *Joseph* and later Jesus were hidden and preserved in Africa, so too was the *Book of Enoch* hidden and preserved in Africa.

Enoch's book was hidden for a period of at least twelve-hundred years. During this time, the world outside of Ethiopia was oblivious to the fact the book was being preserved by the Falasha Jews of Ethiopia. Fortunately for the *Book of Enoch*, the Falasha Jews and Orthodox Christians were themselves quite isolated from the people of the Mediterranean world for a long time.

Re-Introduced to the World

Since then, the *Book of Enoch* has passed through several phases during a prolonged time of its reemergence. In the 19th century there were a number of complete translations, making the book's message available to a wider audience. The translations of R.L. Laurence, G.H. Schodde and R.H. Charles are still widely available. Of notable mention here, is the almost forgotten 1839 translation by John Baty. John Baty was to the 19th century what Whiston had been to the 18th... John Baty's translation includes a lengthy defense of *Enoch's* book as valid for inclusion in our Bibles. Baty's style of prose and verse is vivid and engaging and a worthy addition to your library.

Authenticated at the Dead Sea

175 years after the *Book of Enoch* had rediscovered in Ethiopia, its message was still discounted by the doubtful who claimed it was a forgery. After all, if the Ethiopic *Book of Enoch* were a forgery, it would not be the first time someone tried to recreate a 'lost book' and foist it off as original. In fact, there had been forgeries of the *Book of Enoch* circulated before. The truth is, without some source of external corroboration, a legitimate air of doubt could have remained.

In the 1950's, all doubts that Ethiopic *Enoch* was the same book quoted by New Testament writers were dispelled by the discovery of the Dead Sea Scrolls. In the Jewish libraries hidden for nearly two millennia, then rediscovered in caves by the Dead Sea, fragments from seven manuscripts of *Enoch* in Aramaic had survived. An additional three fragments of Greek copies of *Enoch* were also found there. These fragments have since been used to authenticate and spot-check the Ethiopic translation of *Enoch*. Since the Dead Sea Scroll libraries have been dated to the three centuries before Christ, we now know Ethiopic *Enoch* was and is the real deal.

Disseminated on the Net

Since the 1990's, the text of the *Book of Enoch* has been freely available on the internet. For the first time in history, the *Book of Enoch* is potentially available to people living anywhere on the planet. Surely the light of the truth contained in the pages of the book *Enoch* wrote is shining brighter with each passing day. It would appear that against all the odds, *Enoch's* prophecy concerning the future ministry of his book is in the process of being realized.

However, that the *Book of Enoch*'s best days are yet future, for its purpose is for a generation to come.

Accepted in the Day of Tribulation

> The words of the blessing of *Enoch*, wherewith he blessed the elect and righteous, who will be living in the day of tribulation, when all the wicked and godless are to be removed. And he took up his parable and said -*Enoch* a righteous man, whose eyes were opened by God, saw the vision of the Holy One in the heavens, which the angels showed me, and from them I heard everything, and from them I understood as I saw, but not for this generation, but for a remote one which is for to come. Concerning the elect I said, and took up my parable concerning them: The Holy Great One will come forth from His dwelling, and the eternal God will tread upon the earth, even on Mount Sinai, and appear from His camp, and appear in the strength of His might from the heaven of heavens. (*Enoch* 1:1-4 RHC)

The prophets of *Israel* from the earliest times, predicted a future time of worldwide trouble that would exceed all other periods of crisis for the world and especially for the descendants of *Jacob*. The prophets have called this period of time by many names. The two most common titles given to the final period of worldwide trouble in scripture are, *"The Day of the Lord"* and *"The Tribulation"*, (or *"Great Tribulation"*). *Enoch* prophesies his book will be a blessing to those living in that *"The Day of Tribulation"*.

How will the *Book of Enoch* become a source of blessing to the elect living in the *Day of Tribulation* in a way which former generations have not experienced?

The Restoration of Enoch

For many there remain pertinent doubts concerning the text of *Enoch* as it has come down to us in our day.

Much of *Enoch's* current problem lies with the trustworthiness of its transmission. Had the book been kept entire and transmitted from generation to generation intact in the Hebrew language, people would be more prone to accept it than in its current state. Because the only complete text of *Enoch* today is the Ethiopic one, and since Aramaic *Enoch* is fragmentary, it leaves room for people like Jozef T. Milik to be skeptical about its reliability. Milik states that since the extensive middle portion of the book, which portrays the *"Son of Man"* sitting in judgment on God's *"Throne of Glory"*, has not been corroborated by fragments from the Dead Sea Scroll caves, that its composition is from the late 3rd century after Christ. Milik does see a Jesus-like Messiah figure in the *Book of Enoch*, and because he does, Milik assumes those portions are of Christian origin.

Fifty years ago the *Book of Isaiah* had a similar credibility problem. Isaiah in our printed Bibles is based upon a Hebrew text from the 9th century AD. Questions about Isaiah's transmission led liberal scholars to pose that Isaiah's text had been corrupted during its transmission over the centuries; liberal scholars of an earlier generation had proposed the Hebrew text of Isaiah had even been corrupted by Christian additions!

The discovery of an essentially complete Hebrew copy of Isaiah in the Dead Sea Scrolls put an end to that speculation when it was discovered it was essentially the same textual tradition for Isaiah that the Jews had been preserving since the destruction of the temple in *Jerusalem*.

In the eyes of many, the credibility of the *Book of Enoch* could be resurrected should a more ancient complete copy of that book be found. Should another cache of ancient books be uncovered in which a complete copy of *Enoch* in Hebrew or Aramaic turns up, the book's perceived importance to salvation history could once again be restored.

The Book of Enoch: Toward the Future

Without a doubt the discovery of a complete, truly ancient copy of the *Book of Enoch* in either Aramaic or Hebrew would be a watershed event in the history of the book. Given the fragmentary state of the *Enoch* manuscripts we now have from the Dead Sea Scrolls, the discovery of a complete *Enoch* scroll in one of the languages of the Jews of ancient *Israel* would be revolutionary for *Enoch* studies.

In this light, readers may be shocked to know that it has been reported such a scroll has already been found.

In "Understanding the Dead Sea Scrolls", Avi Katzman writes,

> Regarding the [Dead Sea] scrolls, [John] Strugnell claims at least four other scrolls have been found that have not yet come to light: 'I've seen, with my own eyes, two.' One of the two is a complete copy of the *Book of Enoch*… These scrolls, like the Temple Scroll, came from Cave 11 at Qumran, according to

Strugnell. The manuscripts are now "somewhere in Jordan. Various people own them. Several of them have been sold to big bankers. They're investments for these people. There's no point in forcing a sale. If they really need cash- as one seems to now- I have the money".

As for the other two scrolls- the ones Strugnell has not seen- '[Lankester] Harding [the director of Jordan's Department of Antiquities] on his death bed told me he'd seen three, only one of which I've seen- so that makes four.'

Strugnell is not concerned that the scrolls may deteriorate before scholars can look at them: "They're all being kept very carefully; no one need worry about them. They're a better investment than anything on the *Israel*i or the New York stock exchanges," he added.[2]

Such a find, if and when it comes forward, could catapult the *Book of Enoch* to a renewed status as a legacy of *Israel* to the world. An ancient copy of the *Book of Enoch* in one of the languages of ancient *Israel* may pave the way for restoring the book's reputation in the eyes of many and to better poise the book to become a resource of blessing for the last generation living during the coming Great Tribulation period.

In that light, we find the following cryptic statement in the *Book of Enoch*,

---

[2] Shanks, H. (1992). Understanding the Dead Sea Scrolls: A Reader from the Biblical Archaeology Review. New York, Random House.

When they write down truthfully all my words in their languages, and do not change or minish ought from my words but write them all down truthfully-all that I first testified concerning them. Then, I know another mystery, that books will be given to the righteous and the wise to become a cause of joy and uprightness and much wisdom. And to them shall the books be given, and they shall believe in them and rejoice over them, and then shall all the righteous who have learnt therefrom all the paths of uprightness be recompensed. (*Enoch* 104:11-13 RHC)

In this passage is *Enoch* simply predicting his book's preservation and survival over the millennia, or is *Enoch* saying that his book will have a startling restoration in the last days?

It is not unreasonable for us to expect to hear of breaking news concerning the *Book of Enoch* given the book's most recent history…

Like a comet on a wide elliptical orbit around the sun, *Enoch* is a book of the Bible seemingly on a wide elliptical orbit around the rest of the Biblical corpus, its orbit at times bringing it back into closer relation with the rest of the canon of Scripture as it is doing now.

ISBN 978-168564451-2

Made in United States
North Haven, CT
28 May 2023

37076810R00085